HISTORY OF CAMP DENNISON
1796 ～ 1956

Waldsmith Museum   Photo by Rob Paris

HISTORY OF CAMP DENNISON
1796 ~ 1956

MARY RAHN SLOANE

Commonwealth Book Company
ST. MARTIN, OHIO

First Published by the Camp Dennison
Historical Committe in 1956. This edition
© 2018 by Commonwealth Book Company.
All rights reserved.
Printed in the United States of America.

TABLE OF CONTENTS

		Page
Chapter I	Big Bottom, 1790-1814	7
Chapter II	Germany, 1814-1861	21
Chapter III	Camp Dennison, 1861-1864	27
Chapter IV	Grand Valley, 1865-1917	38
Chapter V	The Methodist Church	69
Chapter VI	Story of the Camp Dennison Schools	87
Chapter VII	Two More Wars — 1917 to Present	101
Chapter VIII	Camp Dennison Today	116
Bibliography		122
Appendix—Headstones in Camp Dennison Cemetery		123
	Copy of Deed to Barbara Landon	127
	Genealogy, Christian Waldsmith Family	127
	Genealogy, Frederick Peckenpaugh Family	133
	Genealogy, The Price Family	137
	Genealogy, The Buckingham Family	139
	Genealogy, Queal Family	146
	Circuit Riders and Preachers, Methodist Church	147
	Sunday School Superintendents, Methodist Church	152

ILLUSTRATIONS

Page

Waldsmith House .....Frontispiece	
Kugler House	9
Enoch Buckingham House	17
Price House	19
Map of Germany - 1844	22
Mr. and Mrs. John Queal	24
Mr. and Mrs. Smith Quayle	24
Picture of Camp Dennison during Civil War	28
Secrest Monument in 1932	35
Dr. Buckingham's House	39
Dr. Alfred Buckingham	40
Mrs. Edna Van Pelt Buckingham	40
Miss Marcia Lucia Buckingham	40
Grocery Store	41
Mt. Olivet Baptist Church	43
Group of Women about 1890	46
Norman Little, Rolf Pinkvoss, John Walsh, Henry Pinkvoss and Duff Boles in front of Knicely's Store	47
Telegraph Station	48
Pennsylvania Railroad Station	56
Henry F. Pinkvoss and Joseph Haffenbradl	62
Methodist Church - 1918	70
Inside of Church	72
Inside of Church, during Sunday School	74
Community House	76
Entrance of Church	78
Allan Wogenstahl at organ of Church	81
Exterior of Methodist Church	83
Miss Bessie Thompson	84
School house prior to 1870	87
Present schoolhouse before remodeling	88
Present schoolhouse - 1956	89
Group pictures of school	93-100
Tennis Court	101
Plaque on Waldschmidt Museum	106
New homes on Lincoln Road	107
Map of Camp Dennison at present time	120-121

FOREWORD

The material presented here took nearly twenty months to assemble in its present form. It is designed first to present the historical background surrounding the one hundred and fiftieth anniversary of the founding of the Camp Dennison Methodist society and its subsequent programs and reunion celebration to be held August 24-26, 1956; second, to present a picture of the village today and such details about the people we have known to interest non-residents; and third, to provide a "jumping off place," as it were, for our successors who will carry on a tradition of regular written supplements and preservation of landmarks.

Many people contributed to this work. Some labored many hours, others took time to answer a question, or reply to a letter, and all offered encouragement. Those quoted in the text are given credit there. Others we must thank are Lola Bonnell, Mrs. Keith Browning, Ruth Peckenpaugh Brunner, Mrs. Nolan Carson, Marie Dickoré, Nellie Falgner, Mrs. William Gant, Lyda Henderson, Earl Howell, Nellie Lewis, Elva Anderson Maphet and Mildred Anderson Bowen, Mrs. H. H. Mathews, Mr. and Mrs. George Malott, Rev. Harold F. Minnich, Mrs. James Morris, Henry M. Pinkvoss, George T. Prather, Mr. and Mrs. Wes Rahn, Hazel Robinson, Julia Buckingham Robinson, Glenn Sloan, Robert Terwillegar and Morris Walton.

The genealogical tables were compiled by Mrs. Rolf Pinkvoss, who wrote the chapter on school history, and Ella Mae Yeager who authored the church history.

INTRODUCTION

The 150th anniversary of the Methodist Church at Camp Dennison, Ohio, provides the occasion for a history of the interesting founding and growth of this community together with brief accounts of some of the men connected with its importance in this part of the Ohio Valley.

We pay tribute to Christian Waldsmith, an American patriot, who had the vision and ability to hew out of the wilderness a settlement and create something of vital and lasting influence. Born March 23, 1755, in Lancaster County, Pennsylvania, he grew up in this region where his father served several churches as pastor. When the Revolutionary War broke out Waldsmith enlisted and fought for his country to the end of the war.

In 1794 he journeyed to the Little Miami valley to investigate the newly opened country in the west. In 1796 he brought a group of his friends and neighbors with their families and settled in the "Big Bottom" of the Little Miami River. Gradually, under his leadership, they built up an empire of mills and business enterprises that almost rivaled Cincinnati. Perhaps the most important of his undertakings were the church and paper mill. Both were vital to the development of this frontier country.

Newspapers and books printed on the paper made at Waldsmith's paper mill are still read and the heritage of the little church has served the people of the valley faithfully throughout the years.

It is in recognition of the foresight and industry of Christian Waldsmith and his group to create something of lasting value that the committee has gathered the information to compile this book in the hope that it will carry forward into the future the story of the achievement of the past.

Marie Dickoré.

Chapter I
"BIG BOTTOM" 1794-1814
Beginners

How they are provided for upon the earth, (appearing at intervals)
How dear and dreadful they are to the earth,
How they inure to themselves as much as to many—
what a paradox appears their age,
How people respond to them, yet know them not,
How there is something relentless in their fate all times,
How all times mischoose the objects of their adulation
And how the same inexorable price and reward must still be paid
for the same great purchase*
—Walt Whitman

The Treaty of Greenville removed from the Ohio country the threat of Indian massacre. Pioneers replaced the frontiersmen as great numbers traveled over the Appalachian Mountains in six-horse Conestoga wagons or by raft or ark drifting down the Ohio River. In the Miami River country the population was not over 2,000 in 1790; in 1800 it was about 15,000. The greater proportion of these were engaged in agriculture. Grist mills converted their wheat into flour; corn was utilized feeding hogs or making whiskey. In the beginning the western pioneers took their flour, bacon, whiskey, pelts and venison to the river settlements to barter for such luxuries of the east as groceries, dry goods and tobacco. River packet lines furnished these importations, also carrying pioneer products further downstream for resale.

CHRISTIAN WALDSMITH was one of a group of Pennsylvanians who came into this fertile but rustic setting in 1794, to examine its business possibilities. The site which satisfied them was a valley three miles long, rich in forests, ten miles above Columbia on the Little Miami River. The greater part of this land passed into the ownership of three men: Christian Waldsmith, Harner, and Levi Buckingham.

Levi Buckingham received by deed from John Cleves Symmes in 1795 the northern part, i.e. Section 14, 20 and 32, in township 5, the "first entire range," in all 1140 acres. For this he paid a dollar an acre. The remaining half of the valley went to Waldsmith, the area of which is not given in the deed, for 3200 Spanish dollars. The deed which Waldsmith received from Symmes read " . . . the said land to be divided by a line drawn from the Little Miami due west across said numbers 13 and 19 so as to make an equal division of quantity . . . the south . . . is hereby conveyed to the said Christian Waldsmith, the other equal north half is to be conveyed to George Harner, also the south half of Section 31 to Waldsmith, and the north half to Harner and the heirs of Conrad Codderman, containing 320 acres in said south half, contents of Sections 13 and 19 to be surveyed hereafter."[1] Harner soon sold his land to Daniel Prisch[2] and Adam Codderman.[3]

The following Pennsylvanians also bought land directly from Symmes: Hans Leckie, 400 acres in Section 14;[4] Thomas Reich, 540 acres in Section 24;[5] Antoni de Golyer, 132 acres adjacent to Leckie's land;[6] and Ludwig Freiberger, 98 acres adjoining Prisch's purchase.[7]

While Waldsmith purchased his tract in 1795, he did not bring his family here until the following year. He was forty-one years old when they moved to Ohio. His wife was Elizabeth Bollender whom he had married in Reading Town, Pennsylvania, August 15, 1785. Before this he had served as a Private in the American Revolution, in the Pennsylvania Regiment, Captain Daniel D. Turch's Co., from Berks County, Pa., Associators.[8] The six children whom they brought with them were between the ages of one and fifteen years.

The following paragraphs are from Thomas Fitzwater's priceless account of the migration.

Fitzwater's Letter[9]

"C. Waldsmith, our own family, and four other families started to this state on or near the first of May, 1796. I have but little recollection of the journey to Juniata, but I recollect that place. The next place I recollect seeing was Bedford Springs. Then nothing more until we came to Redstone. Here we were detained nearly three weeks waiting for our flatboats. At Pittsburgh we met Gen. Wayne's regular army. I have a distinct recollection of seeing the soldiers fire the cannon; then the drum would beat and the fife would play a short time. The army was then going to Erie. Gen. Wayne died the next October. A day or two after leaving Pittsburgh, Chris. Waldsmith was walking on a sandbar when he picked up a fife which looked very ancient. The brass on the ends was black and corroded, and it was full of sand. It was supposed it had been in the river since Braddock's defeat, nearly forty-one years. I saw the fife hundred of times in after years. They lent it to an old revolutionary fifer, and never recovered it again.

"The Ohio was low, and the three flatboats had great difficulty in getting along. They only traveled in the day time, always tying up to the shore at night. At the mouth of the Bracken River two families left and went into Kentucky. After being on the river seven weeks we landed at Columbia. The

Miami was pouring out muddy water and driftwood. This was the first sight I got of that river.

"Not far above the mouth of the Miami the boat which contained Waldsmith's family ran aground. The four men and a boy tried to get it afloat that afternoon and into the night, but they did not succeed. The next morning another boat came along, when they hailed the inmates for assistance; this boat landed close to ours, and I recollect seeing three or four going to the boat which was aground; in two or three hours the boat was afloat. About twenty years ago Father Durham told me the same story, and further said that Waldsmith was so pleased to get his boat afloat that he told them he would give them ten gallons of whiskey for their services. They brought a keg which held three gallons, and he filled that."

It was in the middle of July when they landed at Columbia. In fifteen or eighteen days, when the Miami lowered, they arrived at their journey's end.

The "Big Bottom" which Waldsmith had chosen is about twenty feet lower than the surrounding land.[10] Into this depression he deflected the river through a millrace and went vigorously to work building a saw mill which cut the tall trees into boards and beams for new homes.

In 1797 a gristmill and two copper distilling vats for making whiskey were being constructed.

It was this year that MATTHIAS KUGLER came into the territory. Young Kugler worked for Waldsmith and in 1798 married his oldest daughter, Catherine Elizabeth.

Kugler House, now the residence of Mr. and Mrs. Glenn Sloan.
Photo by Rob Paris.

Three buildings of this era are still standing. Two of the houses are of fieldstone, built after the manner of the "Pennsylvania Dutch" style of Lancaster County, Pennsylvania, their builder's birthplace. The larger stone house bore the inscription "C. Waldsmith-1804" (Illus. 49, No. 4). The smaller stone house (Illus. 49, No. 2) is not dated but it seems natural that Waldsmith would have built a small house first, moving into a large one as he accumulated more wealth. Some people hold the belief that the smaller home was built for Catherine and Matthias Kugler when they were married . . . but this was in 1798, even before the accepted date of the "'parent" house. However, for convenience, it will hereafter be referred to as the "Kugler House." If it *was* constructed 1797-1804, it is the second oldest building still standing in Hamilton County, the oldest being the Suydam house in Sedamsville.

The third extant dwelling is of wood, set between those of stone. Two others like it were originally on either side of the existing one. Mill workers lived in the frame houses.

Almost directly across the street from the Kugler house was a distillery; it was enlarged and used as a barn during the present century and was once shaded by a tall silo at its western end. This (distillery) barn is in the process of being wrecked by Hamilton County so that the site and material may be used for other purposes.

Whiskey, beef, pork, lumber and staves were being shipped from Cincinnati to New Orleans as early at 1803 and a good share of the produce of Waldsmith's mills was among them. It was in connection with this traffic that the Miami Exporting Company was organized under charter from the new state of Ohio. Naturally enough Waldsmith was one of the first board of eleven elected directors of the company. Operating under a very liberal charter, the company also employed some of its capital in banking. The business carried on fairly well until 1822, and finally expired before its forty-year charter terminated. The "bank's" office, near the wharf, one hundred feet west of Sycamore Street in Cincinati, later became a financial center.[11]

We see in the newspaper *Liberty Hall* of September 13, 1809, that a fulling (cloth finishing) business was added to the Waldsmith establishments.

FULLING BUSINESS

The subscriber has lately repaired his fulling mill in the best manner and hopes to be able to render better satisfaction than formerly. He has employed a gentleman from Lexington who understands the (fulling) of cloth well and will give due attendance to all who will favor him with their custom.

Peter Waldsmith

N.B. Where money is (scarce) wheat will be received

in payment when the cloth is dressed and delivered. August 29, 1809.[11]

Peter was Christian Waldsmith's son, then twenty-six years of age. That the business had been repaired may mean it previously had been devastated by flood.

THE MANUFACTURING OF PAPER

Flax was one of the agricultural products of the territory at this time. We know that women spun the threads from which linen clothing and sheets were made, and according to the census of Hamilton County in 1810 a total of 45,913 yards of linen were spun on 329 looms in townships adjacent to Waldsmith's settlement. This census does not mention a paper mill, indicating it was not yet in operation.

Miss Marie Dickoré has examined countless newspapers and family records to discover the facts of this development. Her detailed account appeared for the first time in the bulletin of the Historical and Philosophical Society of Ohio.[12] From it we learn the following facts:

When the papermill at Redstone burned in 1810, the paper shortage in this area became critical. Exasperated lawyers, printers, publishers and storekeepers were dependent upon an imported supply of paper which varied with the state of the Ohio River, and they pressed Waldsmith to set up a paper mill on the Little Miami. The first of many notices of his intentions appeared in *Liberty Hall*, Cincinnati, Ohio, January 16, 1810:

> RAGS WANTED
> C. WALDSMITH
>
> Having commenced the building of a PAPER MILL, on the Little Miami, respectfully informs the public that STORE GOODS will be given for any quantity of clean linen and cotton rags at 3 cents a pound.
>
> RAGS will also be received in payment of book accounts
>
> Those who wish to make special contracts for the delivery of RAGS please to apply immediately.
> January, 1810.

It took Waldsmith a full year to set up vats, assemble rags and find a master paper maker to oversee operations. Finally a large enough stock of paper was on hand to supply the first customer, the newspaper *Western Spy* of Cincinnati, Ohio.

John Smith from Kentucky was the skilled craftsman who supervised the work of putting the mill into operation. He continued for many years as its head vatsman and dryloft boss. He died in Danville, Illinois, aged eighty-five years.

Notices in *Western Spy* and *Liberty Hall* subsequently advertised for boys and girls (of good moral character) as apprentices in the paper making business, offering the boys one hundred dollars in cash, a suit of clothes worth twenty-five dollars when free, and nine months schooling in the time.

Another article in the issue of *Liberty Hall* of December 1, 1811, announced:

CHRISTIAN WALDSMITH

is now preparing in his paper mill another vat and will employ some experienced hands, who understand to work at the vat in the PAPER MAKING BUSINESS. Such will find encouragement at his Mill on the Little Miami.

Also an old man, who is able to teach a night school of reading, writing and arithmetic and in the daytime do some labor — will also find employment.

Storekeepers may be supplied with all kinds of PAPER at the store of Baum and Perry, Cincinnati, — or at the Mill.

Dec. 1, 1811.

A church is marked on the 1844 map of the Waldsmith settlement. The story of this church is found in Chapter V following.

The livelihood of the pioneers did allow for the Sabbath, but other days men rose before dawn and labored until and after dark, making most of their tools and clothing, as well as raising foods and cash crops. The recreational aspects of life, leisure time as we know it, did not exist for them. We who live one hundred and fifty years later find it hard to imagine the difficulties of pioneer life.

Farmers raised or hunted their own meat, supplying their own needs for dairy products and vegetables. In the evenings they made farm implements, clothing, or staves and barrels which could be sold to Waldsmith who used them to haul flour to the shipping lines in Cincinnati. In Waldsmith's new home nearly half of the lower floor had a separate entrance and was used as a general store. We can imagine that a general store with a distillery across the street was a favorite meeting place for the farmers. When Sam told Molly he had to hitch up the team and take the corn to be milled or deliver barrels at Chris's place, he was probably aware that a cup of cheer and friendly conversation around the stove would be available while the work was being done.

Harry Keller, who lives near Milford, possesses account books from this store. Mr. Keller is the great-grandson of John

Keller, Waldsmith's nephew who came here in 1800 to work as a clerk in the general store. When John Keller married Prudence Bell in 1810, they made their home in the small stone house (Illus. 49, No. 2).

Mr. Keller has compiled from these Waldsmith ledgers the following lists of barrel makers, their total output which was sold to Waldsmith in the years 1812-13, and the cash earned by each for his product.

Danl Snell	1841	702.15 5/6
Eli Elston	1312	498.59 1/6
John Snell	1198	399.00
Isac Elston	540	216.66 2/3
James Jones	318	127.20
Ben Dongen	316	118.21 2/3
Ebenezer Osborn	232	90.82 1/2
Adam Snell	133	53.20
Wm. Skillinger	128	51.20
Aaron Matson	125	41.66 2/3
Adam Snell Jr.	85	34.00
John Irwin	65	25.87 1/2
Jno. Straub	39	15.60
James McCollum	10	4.20
15 men employed by John Elston	22	7.33 1/3
	6364	$2,385.73 1/3

33 1/3 cents was paid for each barrel until December 1812; the price was then raised to 37 1/2 cents.

These figures are significant insofar as they show us the practice of a handicraft as well as the quantity of flour Waldsmith must have milled to have filled these barrels. Each barrel held 200 pounds of flour, the 6,364 barrels holding 1,272,800 pounds, or 636.4 tons in two years.

These account books, listing names as well as purchases of customers also provide us with a roster of early residents: Samuel Bockenheim (later Buckingham), _____ Buckingham, Joseph Boone, Antoni de Golyer, Howard Codderman, Andreas Frei (later Fry), Ludwig Freiberger, George Harner, Thomas Haire (Hare), Mathias Kern, Johannes Kugler, William Landon, Hans Leckie, Jacob Leferber, Jacob Lydrich or Lydick, Hans Maddern, Johannes Montag, _____ Muench, Chris Ogg, Andreas Orth (Andrew Orr), Frederick Beckenbach (Peckenpaugh), Daniel Prisch (Price), _____ Radabaugh (Redenbaugh), Hans Robe, David Snider, Kasper Spaeth, Val Weigans, Ludwig Weller, _____ Yost. Other names in the store records indicate that traders came from a distance of ten miles to buy, sell and use the mill facilities.

Of all commodities, cash was the most scarce. An average day's wages was fifty cents, just the price of a package of pins. The general store did not handle much food. We find the following items mentioned:

Tea ($3.00/lb.) — probably saved for "company" — loaf sugar (37¢/lb.), green coffee beans, chocolate, salt, lard and whiskey (37¢/qt.), snuff, buttons, ribbon, silk, muslin, pewter, dishes, bottles, bar iron, fish hooks and ammunition.

Roads, over which wagons engaged in commerce, were at this time in deplorable condition. After the War of 1812 some turnpikes were built because of our new interest in military security, and by 1825 the northern section of the Miami Valley was connected with the eastern states. This was the age of toll roads and canals, but most of these were directed toward Cincinnati.

The difficulty of traveling caused Waldsmith's store to be used as a bank of sorts. Money was often left with the clerks to be repaid a lender when he appeared in the store, thus saving the borrower from traveling a distance to repay it personally.

The Washington Survey Purchase

On March 25, 1811, Waldsmith bought from Joseph Kerr 1060 2/3 acres of land on the eastern bank of the Little Miami, above the mouth of the East Fork River in Clermont County. The price was 619 barrels of super-fine flour. A portion of the property is now the Boys Scouts' Camp Friedlander. On this land stands the ancient "Neville Cabin" near Harner's Run. A copy of this deed recently found among Kerr's papers is written on paper bearing the watermark "Miami W & Co."[14] Trees cut on this tract may have been allowed to drift down the river to the big dam Waldsmith built at the entrance to the mill race, thence into the race and to the sawmill. The clear limestone water that filled the Little Miami from creeks such as Harner's Run helped make a fine white paper such as Waldsmith's mill produced.

This land that Joseph Kerr sold to Waldsmith was originally one of George Washington's three land holdings in Clermont County.

Two more children were born in Ohio to Christian and Catherine: David and Catherine. Three of their eight children had died, and little Catherine was only four years old when the mother died in November, 1810.

We believe Catherine Bollender Waldsmith is buried in the Camp Dennison cemetery, possibly in the unmarked grave at the side of Waldsmith.

In 1811, when he was fifty-six years old, Waldsmith married

Magdalena (Polly) Kern Custard, a thirty-three year old widow. Their daughter Sarah was born the following year.[15]

Waldsmith's Death

Both Waldsmith and his son John died during an epidemic of influenza in March, 1814. His obituary appeared in *Liberty Hall* April 12, 1814:

> DIED at his house on the Little Miami on the 31st ult. CHRISTIAN WALDSMITH. An industrious, enterprising citizen, he has for some years been a very useful member of the community—incessantly engaged in the erection of grist mills, a fulling mill and paper mill—all of which are now in successful operation and highly beneficial to the surrounding country.

The notice of administration appeared in the *Western Spy*, Cincinnati, Ohio, April 26.

NOTICE

All persons indebted to the estate of Christian Waldsmith, late of Sycamore township, Hamilton County, either by bond, note or bank account, are hereby notified to come forward and make payment immediately—and all persons making demands against said estate, are requested to bring them forward legally attested for settlement on or before the fifth day of April next. Public notice is also given, that on Monday, the 16th of May next, will be exposed for sale on the farm of Christian Waldsmith, dec'd., all the personal property belonging to said estate to wit—Store goods consisting of dry goods, groceries, hardware, bar iron, a quantity of whiskey, two stills with the vessels be-belonging thereto, horses, cows, sheep, hogs, farming utensils, bedsteads, beds and bedding, household and kitchen furniture, one set of blacksmith tools, 2 wagons and gears, also wood work of a new wagon, rye in the stack, corn and rye in the mill, wheat and rye in the ground, and an elegant eight day clock. Likewise the gristmill and blacksmith shop to rent. Liberal credit will be given, by giving notes and approved security-terms made known on day of sale. The sale to continue from day to day until all be sold.

Due attendance given by

                                        Jno Keller)
                                        Peter Bell) Adm's.

Apr. 14, 1814.

Peter Bell and John Keller, appointed administrators of the estate, property in Columbia, Cincinnati and the county, were bonded at $80,000.[15] The value of these would have been about $40,000, as it was the custom to bond at twice an estate's worth.

Waldsmith accomplished in this raw territory what usually required the energies of several men. The store, the mills and the church all provided a basis for the civilization that was soon to change the appearance of the Indians' land. And his paper helped immeasurably in a critical era when without paper news could not have been distributed, surveyors' measurements had to be carved on bark with a knife, and letters could not have been written . . . paper is the bloodstream of enterprise.

The name of "Montauk," once applied to Route 126, is evidently derived from "Montag" — Johannes Montag, already mentioned as one of the earliest settlers — as the German pronunciation of the man's last name would yield our American spelling of Montauk.

Buckingham Road on Indian Hill quite possibly marked the boundary of Enoch or Levi Buckingham's property, or perhaps one of their later descendants.

"Harner's Run," of course, is the creek that runs through Camp Edgar Friedlander, and land once belonging to George Harner, before emptying into the Little Miami River.

The Peckenpaughs, the Boones, the Cunninghams, the Buckinghams, the Prices, and Many Others

We have followed the Waldsmith story closely so far, but have no intention of neglecting those other pioneers whose names appeared in the roster selected from Waldsmith's store records. While their industry did not bring these people such great fame, they and their progeny have been a part of us throughout these fifteen decades.

Starting with the PECKENPAUGHS (or Beckenbachs, or Peckinpaughs or Peckingpaughs — the church records and family Bible spell it every conceivable way), we can see from the following lists that members of the family married Boones, Buckinghams, Cunninghams, and Prices, all residents of "Germany": marrying the girl next door was handier when courting was done by young men who probably found their means of transportation, the faithful horse, quite lazy after being hitched to a plow twelve hours a day.

The first Frederick and Elizabeth Peckenpaugh were Pennsylvanians who raised eight children in Ohio. The original homestead was on Cunningham Road and is now owned by Mrs. Chester Kroger. Frederick Jr. lived on the same site and he and his family were active in the Methodist Church. He was one of the trustees who supervised the moving of the church to its present Jackson Street location. His son, Charles, who had a good bass voice and loved to sing, lead the singing and was Sunday School superintendent several times.

You will notice that the Terwilleger brothers who married Peckenpaugh sisters were sons of John and Catherine Buckingham Terwilleger. The whole of that family may be seen in the Terwilleger genealogy.

The CUNNINGHAMS' first purchase lay along the road which now bears that name on Indian Hill. William lived on the northern side of the road, and his brother Albert on the south. Albert J. Cunningham was elected to the Ohio State Legislature in 1869 where he served as Speaker of the House. His children attended the Methodist Sunday School until they moved to Cincinnati. (Continued in Appendix, Table II).

Two BUCKINGHAM brothers, Levi and Enoch, sons of William Buckingham (a Revolutionary soldier of Pennsylvania), settled in our valley about 1789 or 1790. Levi came first and then sent for his brother. They owned the upper part of the valley across the river from Miamiville and their property extended south to the Price holdings. A picture of the house originally built by Enoch Buckingham is included in this book,

Enoch Buckingham house at the end of Myers' Lane, also called the Paxton house.

however the house itself is to a great extent torn down. Only the walls of the lower floor are standing at this time but this enables one to see the type of construction. It was a log house covered with claphoard on the outside and plastered on the inside. There was a large fireplace in the kitchen and another one on the second floor just above the kitchen.

At one time there were many descendants of the Buckingham brothers living in this area, the best known one being Dr.

Alfred Buckingham. He maintained his residence and practiced medicine in the village until his death in 1912. He was a brilliant man and everyone who knew him has a favorite story to tell about him.

At the present time only the following descendants of the Buckingham brothers live here: Mrs. Julia Buckingham Robinson, who is the only surviving descendant carrying the name of Buckingham, Mrs. Florence Fletcher Pinkvoss, who is a great granddaughter of Levi Buckingham through her father, Hall Fletcher; Shirley Quayle, grand daughter of Smith Quayle; and John Queal, son of William Queal.

Some members of the Levi Fletcher family (Levi was a brother of Hall Fletcher) lived here until 1954 when Wilbur and his daughter, Vonnie, moved away. (Continued in Appendix).

William, David and Jesse FLETCHER, natives of Pennsylvania, first settled in 1791 in Clermont County, Ohio, in the neighborhood of Stonelick Creek. In 1801 they moved on farms in the same county which were later owned by Henry Balzhizer, J. W. Robinson and Philip Gatch. William built and owned distilleries and sawmills, two industries that were always needed in that early economy.[17]

When the Fletchers moved to Hamilton County, William W. married Lydia Buckingham, the daughter of Levi. Their first log cabin was built on the homestead which is still owned by their grandchildren. In 1859 they moved into the farmhouse they had built and which is still standing. The log cabin was torn down later. They had ten children, most of whom are buried with their parents in the Miamiville, Ohio, cemetery. (Continued in Appendix).

Daniel PRISCH (Price) came here in 1800 with his children, Nimrod, Abigail and Jeremiah. The Prices owned most of this particular valley north of Waldsmith's property and south of Buckingham's. Nimrod was established on this side of the river and Jeremiah was given the property just across the river in Clermont County. There is a story handed down through the family that Daniel declared he separated the two boys because one was a Methodist and one a Universalist and he wanted to keep them from fighting.

Jeremiah and his wife became members of the Methodist Society organized near Milford, Ohio, at the residence of Rev. Philip Gatch, and later was a local preacher in this area. His great grandson, W. E. Price of Mulberry, Ohio, has in his possession a small document licensing him as a local preacher and signed by W. Herr, Presiding Elder, August, 1857. On this form he is called an "Exhorter." Jeremiah had 13 children (see genealogy). His youngest son, Jeremiah, Jr. was born in 1835.

The family crossed the river to attend services at our church as Jeremiah Jr. united with the M. E. Church at Camp Dennison in 1867 under the pastorate of Rev. Rutledge.

Old Price house at end of Zumstein Lane.   Photo by Rob Paris.

Nimrod and Rachel Peckenpaugh Price had ten children, all of whom must have lived for some time in the village as there are many houses designated as Price houses. The detailed genealogy of this branch of the family is listed in the Appendix. William P. Price, the youngest son, lived in town until he died in 1932, and is well remembered by many of the present residents. During the last years of his life he carried the mail from the post office to the railroad station where it was picked up by the Pennsylvania Railroad.[18]

*From *Leaves of Grass* by Walt Whitman, Copyright 1924 by Doubleday & Company, Inc.
1. After Ratterman: Hamilton County Plat Books Vol. C.1, p. 332.
2. Ibid., Vol. C.1, p. 332.
3. Ibid., Vol. C.1, p. 163.
4. Ibid., Vol. B.2, p. 439.
5. Ibid., Vol. F.1, p. 13.
6. Ibid., Vol. K., pp. 62 and 228.
7. This deed is not recorded but a deed from Freiberger to Peckinpaugh is entered in Book F.2, p. 428.
8. Pennsylvania Archives, 5th Series, Vol. 5, p. 139 (Marie Dickoré).
9. *History of Clermont County, Ohio, 1795-1880*, compiled by J. L. Rockey and R. J. Bancroft and others, publ. by Louis H. Everts, Philadelphia, Pa., 1880. pp. 461-2.
10. The name "Big Bottom" is found on letters addressed to persons living in this settlement, as: "John Keller, Big Bottom, Little Miami, Milford, Ohio." This kind of address, plus the fact the son-in-law-successor to Waldsmith, Matthias Kugler, had many business interests in Milford, may have been the reason many writers speak of industries in the Big Bottom settlements being "the Kugler mills in Milford."
11. *Memoirs of the Miami Valley*, Vol. 2, Ed. by W. C. Culkins; Robert O. Law Company, Chicago, 1919, pp. 632-33.
12. Harry Keller's records.

13. *Bulletin*, Historical and Philosophical Society of Ohio, Vol. 5, No. 1, March, 1947.
14. Newspaper clippings. Miss Marie Dickoré, Cincinnati Times-Star, June 26, 1940 and February 22, 1941.
15. Ruth Voorheis Matthews, of Findlay, Ohio, is Magdalena Kern's great-great-niece. Her interest in tracing these family records has aided our efforts considerably. Mrs. Matthews believes the second Mrs. Waldsmith may be buried in or near Montgomery County, Ohio, as she seemed to have been there in 1850 as the wife of Lain Ready.
16. Hamilton County Court Records.
17. *History of Clermont County, Ohio.* Op.cit., p. 520.
18. We are indebted to Jessie Price Lytle of St. Petersburg, Florida, the daughter of William P. Price, for information on the Nimrod Price family, and particularly comments regarding the different houses in the village. The data on the Jeremiah Price family was obtained from Mr. W. E. Price of Mulberry, Ohio, and the Price family Bible which he has in his possession.

Chapter II

"GERMANY" 1814-1861

Waldsmith died without leaving a will, and in the administration of his estate each of the children received an equal share of the property. His son-in-law Matthias Kugler made a career for himself in the business world, and his name is well known. As matters adjusted themselves, Matthias Kugler and his son John took over some of the mills, including the paper mill. It was then that the watermark was changed from "Miami-W & Co." to "M. Kugler & Son." The paper mill burned in 1848-50. Henry Clay Smith, the son of the mill's first operator, John Smith, made the last sheet of paper.

The Kugler interests gradually moved to neighboring Milford, Ohio, where the family home is still a landmark, now being a restaurant known as "Millcroft Inn."

The Kugler Mill Road leads from Indian Hill to the site of "Germany," following the course of a creek called "Flat Run." Nearing the two cone shaped hills standing between it and the river, the creek turns to the right, thence to the Little Miami; whereas the road bears left toward the mill site. It is to be regretted that an attempt has been made to change the historic name of Kugler Mill Road in recent years.

The still limited means of communication spurred the development of railways. Notwithstanding the great need and the liberal granting of charters by the state, railroads suffered freely from abandonment and financial strangulation. In the 1840's, flour mills were making 100,000 pounds of flour per year along the Little Miami River, and twenty-six saw mills and three paper mills were operating.

Contracts were let by the Little Miami Railroad Company for lumber for the superstructure of fifteen miles of road to Kugler Mills after 1837.[1] In September, 1840, a contract for the "graduation" of ten miles of road bed above Kugler Mills (through Miamiville) was made.

John Kugler subscribed $10,000 to the stock of the company on condition that the survey run within eighty rods of his mills. Thus, the fourteen miles beyond Milford including the bridge across the river at Miamiville just above Camp Dennison were finished and put into use December 1, 1842.

Older residents mention that the rails originally were on a trestle over the valley of "Germany." A land fill later replaced this trestlework.

On the early railroads oak stringers, covered with a 5/8" thickness of strap iron were used as rails. The first coaches

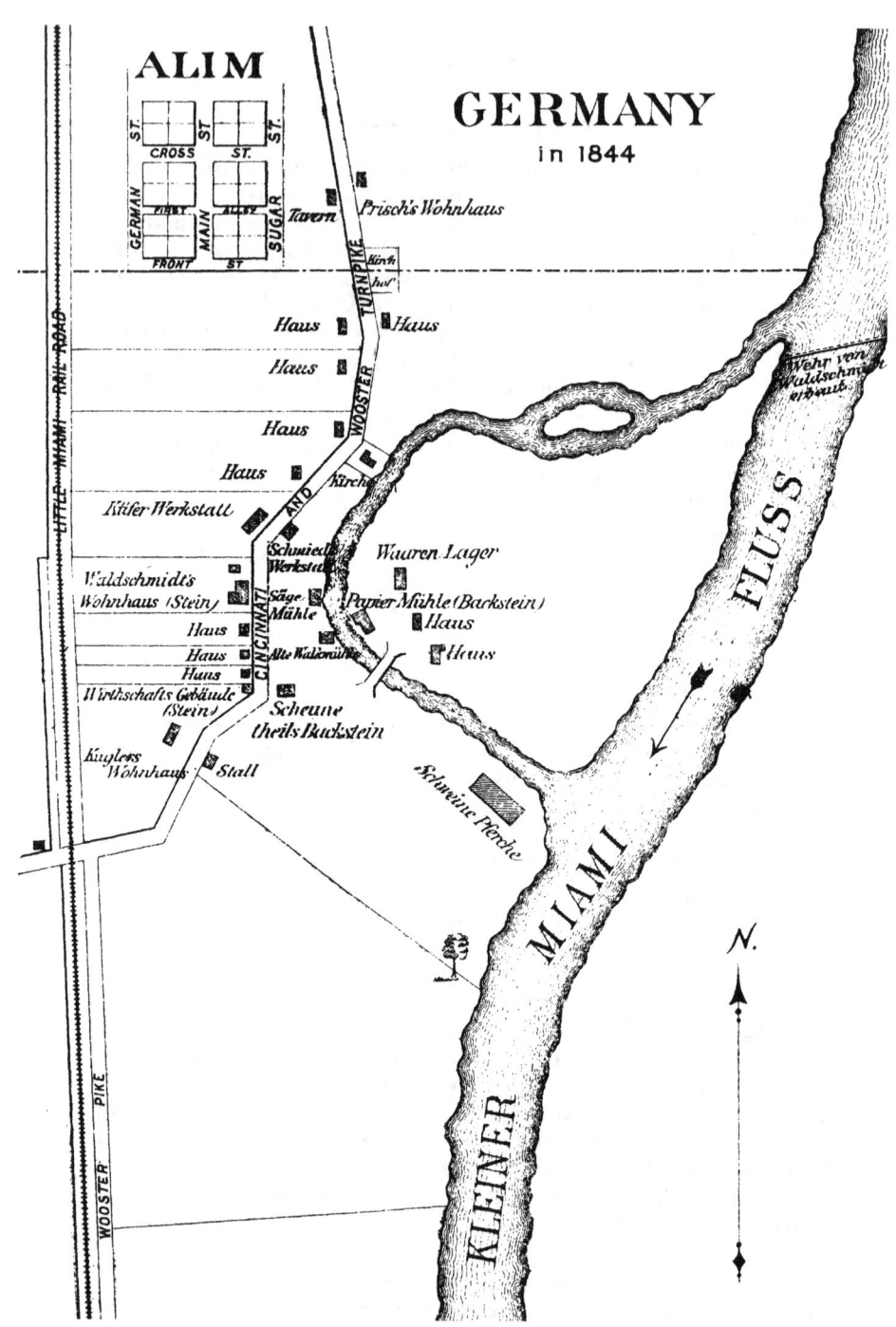

closely followed the design of the early stage coaches, with a double deck arrangement seating about twenty-four persons. The first engines were similar in constrution to those used in threshing machines and weighed only ten tons including fuel and water. The speed of these craft was about ten miles per hour for passengers, and half that for freight, and charges were as high as twenty-five cents the ton mile. Even so, the two trains in operation were known as "The Flyer" and "The Express."[2]

This railroad brought "Germany" within the sphere of influence of Cincinnati. Rather than aiding in the development of the smaller community, it must have brought these industries into keen competition with others, because when some of the mills burned in 1848, they were not rebuilt. Matthias Kugler died in 1854; the paper mill had already been closed. Gradually, the thriving community disintegrated. Today the powerful diesels of the Pennsylvania Railroad Company, which had leased the rails of the Little Miami Company, pass through "Germany" without consideration of the once famous Waldsmith empire.

We are afforded a relief from verbal description by this map which was entered in the Hamilton County courthouse in 1844. It is a map of "Germany," the name chosen for the tiny town on Waldsmith's land, showing some of the houses and mills, the railroad and the Wooster Turnpike, which ran from Cincinnati to Columbus where it connected with the Pike built from Wooster.

In 1843 Nimrod Price laid out the town of Alim at the southern edge of his farm.

Alim, now part of Camp Dennison, never materialized although some cottages used to be located along the above streets. The names of Pinkvoss Lane, Lincoln Road and Route 126 are now used on some of the old Alim roads. This practice of laying out a town on a large land purchase was not uncommon among early farmers. Pleasant Plain, Ohio, originated this way.[3]

The QUEAL family, while not among the first settlers in this community, have always been important in the church history as various members of this family have been mainsprings of the Methodist Church until recent years. Michael Queal and his wife, Louise Mytilla Moore, came first to Milford, Ohio, and bought a distillery. In 1835 they bought the Queal farm which is now owned by the Gant family. Henry (W. H.) Queal was postmaster for many years and lived on Cunningham Road (Res. No. 84, Illus. 49). George W. Queal lived on the home farm and later moved to California and Maria Queal Connett lived on the Queal farm across the road from the Indian Hill Water Works where Mrs. Pearl Queal and her son John are living at the present time.

John O. Queal attended the Camp Dennison School and with the outbreak of the war between the North and the South, enlisted in 1861, in Company G, First Ohio Calvary. He served for four years and was discharged as a sergeant. He and Jennie Buckingham were married around 1867 in the Methodist

Mr. and Mrs. John O. Queal

Mr. and Mrs. Smith Quayle at their 50th Wedding Anniversary at the church.

Church before it was moved to its present location. He and his family lived on the Queal farm across the little Miami River from Miamiville, Ohio. Smith B., his son, who changed the spelling of his name to Quayle, graduated from Ohio Wesleyan University and subsequently worked on the Enquirer, the Times-Star, Cincinnati Post Office, the Free Press, Crowell Publishing Co. and the Phil Morton Advertising Co. He married

Emma Cottingham of Cincinnati in 1890, also a graduate of Ohio Wesleyan, and they were well known by many residents still living here. Smith Quayle knew more about the church than any of the recent members and it is to be regretted that the records which were in his possession when he died in 1943 have disappeared. He and Mrs. Emma Quayle were leaders in the church until their deaths. He was also on the Camp Dennison School Board, as was Matson, his son, and he was president of the Symmes Township Sunday School Association for many years. During the years 1887, 1888 and 1889 Smith B. Queal is listed in the Conference records as "local preacher." A well remembered remark of Mrs. Emma Quayle was that she liked it when anyone called her a crank "because a crank made things go."[5] Matson died in March 1956. (See Appendix)

The Henry STROMAN family must have been influential in our village, however little information can be secured about them. Our available records state that the first Methodist Society meeting was held in Henry Stroman's cottage but it is not known where this was located. However, the James Stroman property was on the west side of Buckingham Road, and is now owned by Warner Atkins. James was the son of Henry and he and his family were active in the Camp Dennison church from 1856 to 1871. Henry Stroman was a trustee of the Milford Methodist Church in 1818 and was a trustee of the Camp Dennison church when it was built in 1845. James Stroman, according to his granddaughter, Mrs. Robert Flinn of Indian Hill, was a Presbyterian minister. He and his wife Phoebe had ten children: Sarah, George, Henry, Martin, Alfred, Polk, Hattie, Almira, Rose and Phoebe Anna. Mrs. Flinn is the daughter of Phoebe Anna Stroman Printy.

Margaret and Thomas WALSH were residents of our village for some years prior to the Civil War. They lived on the west side of the main highway near the Miamiville Bridge; their house later was destroyed by flood. They had four children, two of whom married and moved away: Ed married Martha Reynolds and Margaret married Thomas McDonough and they had six children. Johnny Walsh is well remembered as station agent for many years. He was born in 1865 and married Maggie Murphy from Milford. They had no children. He worked for the Pennsylvania Railroad all of his life, first as a watchman for the bridge and then as station agent. His wife preceded him in death by many years, and later his sister Mamie lived with him in the house on Cunningham Road (Res. 84, Illus. 49). Johnny Walsh died in 1940 and Mamie then moved to the city where she died in 1942.[6]

Mr. and Mrs. Nicholas FAUL moved here with their baby daughter Julia, from Butler, Kentucky, in 1859. Rosa was born in the Kugler house that year. Willie, a third child, died when he was sixteen. Julia, who married John Nash, died in 1944. Rosa married Charles EDSALL and had one daughter, Fannie, who married Chester Brown and lives in Lancaster, Ohio. Mrs. Edsall became Mr. Henry Queal's housekeeper after Mr. Edsall's death, and took over the post office in 1907. While she operated the post office, it was located in the home she built on Clement Street (No. 95, Illus. 49). She also had the library in this building.[7]

1. *Memoirs of the Miami Valley*, publ. by Robert O. Law Co., Chicago, Ill., 1919, pp. 156-58.
2. *The Little Miami Railroad* — Robert L. Black, Cincinnati, Ohio, pp. 20, 29, 33, 42.
3. Map taken from *Germany* by Ratterman.
4. *The History of Pleasant Plain, Ohio*, by Nelson Stewart; publ. by Benj. F. Klein, Cincinnati, Ohio, 1952.
5. Information obtained from Milford Cemetery, old deeds to Queal property, and *Memoirs of the Miami Valley*, Vol. III, Biographical, Hamilton County, publ. by Robert O. Law Co., Chicago, Illinois.
6. Information obtained from Miss Catherine McDonough, daughter of Margaret Walsh McDonough, Cincinnati, Ohio.
7. Information obtained from Mrs. Fannie Edsall Brown, Lancaster, Ohio.

Chapter III

CAMP DENNISON 1861-1864

In order to justify the study of history, we have only to picture the plight of the amnesia victim who has to find his way without knowledge of the past. It is obvious that to take an intelligent part in our society the citizen should know how it came to be, he should understand how its ills evolved, that he might seek to correct them, and how its virtues developed, that he might better preserve and strengthen them.

Irwin Abrams
(From Antioch Notes)

The next historical phase was the one which left us with that name which still puzzles the passer-by: Camp Dennison.

"What kind of a camp?" is the usual query.

The need for maintaining protective military posts in and around Cincinnati during the War between the States was obvious from its proximity to the "border," and also because it would be an important recruiting center, drawing not only on its urban community but all the surrounding counties.

It had become increasingly apparent that the industrial north and the "small-farmer" western states were moving so fast in population and productiveness that their political influence would weigh against the needs of the South's cotton economy. (The whiskey, pork, lumber, and flour that we noted earlier were being shipped down the Ohio River found a ready market in states where the crop had become specialized.) The South was in sullen fury but compromise after compromise followed days of debate and the Union held together until the outspoken Lincoln, who called slavery "a moral, a social and a political wrong," was elected. In his inaugural address Lincoln was conciliatory but insistent in his intention of preserving the Union. Two days later President Davis called for 100,000 Confederate troops. On April 14, 1861, cannon spoke over Charleston Harbor.

The records of the War Department in the National Archives indicate that Camp Dennison, Ohio, was established in May, 1861, as a Depot for the Volunteer Recruiting Service. It was also used as a general hospital and as a rendezvous for returning troops awaiting muster out of the service at the close of the Civil War. The post was discontinued in September, 1865.

A partial list of the post commanders appears below.

NAME	RANK	FROM	TO
M. S. Wade	Brig. Gen.	Nov. 20, 1861	March. 1862
		March 1862	Aug. 23, 1862

Henry M. Judah	Brig. Gen.	Aug. 23, 1862	Sept. 5, 1862
Edward V. Brookfield	Captain	Sept. 1862	Dec. 1862
Jacob Ammen	Brig. Gen.	Dec. 1862	Jan. 1863
A. J. Ware	Captain	Jan. 1863	Jan. 15, 1863
George W. Neff	Lt. Col.	Jan. 15, 1863	July 24, 1863
Mason Brayman	Brig. Gen.	July 24, 1863	Jan. 1864
William D. Hamilton	Colonel	Jan. 31, 1864	Feb. 3, 1864
Robert H. Bentley	Lt. Col.	Feb. 3, 1864	March 1864
William Von Doehn	Captain	Mar. 25, 1864	May 19, 1864
Caleb Marker	Colonel	May 1864	May 1864
George W. Barrere	Lt. Col.	May 31, 1864	June 1864
A. L. Whiteman	Major	June 9, 1864	June 10, 1864
William Von	Captain	Oct. 1864	Nov. 17, 1864
Edward F. Noyes	Colonel	Nov. 17, 1864	Mar. 29, 1865
Darius B. Warner	Lt. Col.	Mar. 29, 1865	May 1865
George L. Andrews	Lt. Col.	May 12, 1865	Sept. 1865

Although the War Department records in Washington include some seventeen hospital registers of the patients confined at Camp Dennison, these do not include reports of its hospital corps. There are also post returns and tri-monthly reports which show names of commissioned officers, whether present or absent, relevant remarks, together with statistical information regarding present and absent non-commissioned personnel. No maps, plans, or drawings showing the layout of the camp or the locations of various buildings are to be found in the Archives.

We can elaborate considerably on this sketch provided by the War Records Branch of the National Archives and Records Service . . . legend, newspaper lore and the memory of Camp Dennison have a great deal more to say about this critical era.

"It was on April 26, 1861, that Manager Clement, of the Pennsylvania Railroad, went to the point . . . and asked the land holders of the immediate vicinity to meet with him the next day and set a rental price on their holdings. The next day Attorney A. E. Ferguson, of Cincinnati, later President of the Cincinnati Southern Railway Trustees, drew up the lease for the land to the State of Ohio. Dr. Alfred Buckingham[1], then a young physician, leased 700 acres to the state. It is said by some that the camp site was laid out under the direction of the famous General Rosecrans, but Dr. Buckingham said an engineer named Cotton, with the Little Miami Railroad, did this. He saw Gen. Rosecrans, then a rising officer, at the camp on one occasion. The first year the camp was used mainly for drill purposes, but after the battle of Pittsburgh Landing in 1862, a hospital was also established. The hospital included 70 wooden barracks, each 120 feet long by 24 feet wide. There were two hundred beds. For two years Dr. Buckingham was in charge of the Seventh Division hospital corps. Major Cloak, of Kentucky, was in charge of the hospital for a considerable time.[2]

A newspaper article written by Frank Y. Grayson, February 28, 1933, had this to say:

"Thirty thousand Northern lads, the majority of them from Ohio, received military training of a more or less sketchy character here. This camp was by far the largest of several military stations devoted to the conversion of raw materials of bench, desk and farm into soldiers in Hamilton County.[3] It was organized at the request of Governor Dennison . . . the site was selected by Gen. W. S. Rosecrans.

"The site was ideal for the purpose, being on a level plain bisected by the Little Miami Railroad. A turnpike ran through the tract, and a towering hill lent itself to the installation of a reservoir.

"Considerable dissatisfaction was aroused by the necessity of the state paying large sums of money for the various leases. The camp was eventually turned over to the Federal government and it was then that it burgeoned into an impressive post.

"Gen. Jacob D. Cox was the first commander of the camp and at the time (April, 1861) it was laid out to accommodate a dozen regiments. Huts were erected for the companies and the soldiers carried the boards on their shoulders from the trains to the sites shown. [The railroad siding paralleled Kilgore Rd. near Lincoln]. These huts were larger structures and there were three or four on each side of a street at the head of which was the officers' quarters. In the rear of the latter were buildings which ensconced the commandant and staff.

"Tents also began to dot the landscape as recruits in large numbers began to arrive. The cavalry regiments were located in the bottoms that stretched away from the river. Some of the companies started to put floors and bunks in their huts and Rosecrans ordered them removed. The soldiers protested vigorously and the whole matter was laid before General Cox with Rosecrans irate because of the mild rebellion against his authority. General Cox's decision favored the soldiers. At the time of the incident the men were not armed and the camp was more or less makeshift.

"Schools were established but the training lessons were confined mostly to marching. On May 20th Gen. Joshua Bates, by virtue of his seniority, became the commandant With him he brought his all-Cincinnati brigade, which included the Fifth, Sixth, Ninth and Tenth Ohio Regiments, all of which were to have the names of many battles in gilded letters on regimental colors before the war was over.

"Measles broke out and women of Cincinnati shared the nursing. The Ninth Ohio was the famous Turner regiment, of Germans, the Tenth was of Irish persuasion. There threatened to be Civil War within the camp itself when the Tenth decided that unusual zeal was being displayed by the military police of the Ninth in filling the guardhouse with exhilarated men of the Tenth, which was commanded by Gen. M. H. Lytle. The Ninth was commanded by Gen. Robert McCook. Both of these distinguished citizens were to die in the service; Lytle at Chicamauga and McCook to be shot by a guerilla while lying helpless in an ambulance . . . ."

A pump house in a shed built on the north side of the Waldsmith home forced water to the reservoir previously mentioned. From the reservoir it flowed into pipes which permeated the camp. Lengths of this pipe have been dug up since that time always affording the excavator a thrilling reminder of the vast organization that formerly crowded the valley with the sight and sound of men at work.

When the pumping operations were discontinued, the bricks lining this reservoir were removed and used in building an addition to William Knicely's store.

Today the old reservoir is just a large hole on the hilltop surrounded by tall trees, gradually eroding and filling with scrub growth, but it can be seen by the energetic walker. This particular hilltop also gives the viewer an entrancing panorama of the little village, as one traces the winding highway and narrow streets eventually losing themselves beneath the deciduous trees which shade the neat white houses.

If a person standing near the reservoir ruin looks to the north, slightly east of where the highway bridge crosses the Little Miami River before entering Miamiville, he will see a very steep cliff. Beyond that hillside is the Boy Scout Camp, Camp Edgar Friedlander. It is said that soldiers practiced firing cannons from these southern hills, across the valley, into the other hillside nearly two miles away. We have heard the target referred to as "Cedar Banks" and "The Devil's Backbone." The latter name seems to be a more fitting description of a jagged outline rising so steeply above the river.

Another precipice is on the western side or the hill included in Camp Ross. This is gradually being covered by a second growth of foliage, but was bared to provide earth for a railroad land fill in Red Bank.

Gallant Daniel McCook, the father of General McCook, was killed in the skirmish with Morgan's raiders. Curiously enough, he was not in the service but was riding with the cavalry as a volunteer. The story of John Morgan's wild ride through Ohio directly involved Camp Dennison.[4]

In July of 1863 Rosecrans was menacing the southern forces at Tullahoma, Gen. Burnside, in Cincinnati, was gathering forces to penetrate into Tennessee. Bragg dispatched his officer, John Morgan, into Kentucky to sever communications between these two parties, thus delaying the possibility of attacks from them. Morgan, however, conceived the idea of entering Northern territory to create panic and draw after him troops that might otherwise be sent to reinforce Rosecrans and Burnside. Crossing the river near Rising Sun, Indiana on the 8th of July, he arrived at Camp Dennison the morning of the 14th. The speed and audacity with which he acted had enabled him to pass at night through the very outskirts of Cincinnati with hardly a skirmish. False rumors and the smugness of the citizenry nearly defeated the force of 50,000 Ohio Militia against a desperate 2,000. The Militia had been summoned as late as the 13th: "All forces residing in Montgomery, Clinton, Warren, Fayette, Ross, Highland and Brown Counties, report forthwith to Colonel Neff, the military commander at Camp Dennison." A picket skirmish ensued at Camp Dennison and the rebel forces burned a park of government wagons, but one of their lieutenants and several privates fell prisoner to the Ohio forces.

A newspaper article appearing in the Cincinnati *Times-Star* in July 1932 relates the story of the wrecking and burning of a Little Miami Railroad locomotive and three coaches near Camp Dennison by Morgan and his raiders.

"J. E. Q. Maddox . . . a boy of seventeen . . . enlisted and started for Camp Dennison (from Hillsboro) running into Morgan's trail on the way. He took the B. & O. train from Hillsboro to Loveland and started to walk six miles to Camp Dennison. Near Miamiville he saw a locomotive and three coaches overturned and ablaze. He discovered that Morgan's raiders had just crossed the Little Miami River. They had wrecked the train—it was a military train carrying a band of musicians going from Columbus to Camp Dennison to join the army . . . He could see some of the musical instruments burning in the fire. . . . Records at Columbus showed that the State paid the sum of $13,700 to the railroad company to cover the loss of the locomotive and three coaches. This was, no doubt, the biggest loss sustained in Hamilton County during the war through any Conferderate action."

Some soldiers, finally assembled after Morgan had gone, hurried by railroad after him. Other militia marched until near Batavia where they halted and began felling trees to hinder the invader in case he decided to return over the same route! It was some time before the defense was able to anticipate Morgan's behavior well enough to dispatch a force to block the road in *front* of him. On July 26, he was finally captured at Salineville, and was imprisoned in the Ohio Penitentiary, as befitting a horse thief, which he was, as he always was exchanging tired for fresh horses in the course of marching. One of these exhausted animals, probably from Kentucky, was found in old Maud's pasture at the Fletcher farm the day Morgan passed by. Fletcher, like everyone else, claimed reparation from the county for losses to the raider,[5] but soon discovered he had an exceptional trotting horse, and was more than compensated by the glossy cups and wagers he brought home thereafter.

Meanwhile, Morgan and six other men were carving their way out of the penitentiary with table knives. A revengeful director had ordered that "the d——d rebels be made to sweep out their own cells," and as the result of such neglect the prisoners tunneled away. They escaped after some months, rode the Little Miami Railroad to the outskirts of Cincinnati, and were straightway concealed and forwarded into Kentucky.

All of this was in vain, however. Rosecrans with 57,000 men was pursuing Bragg who received reinforcement, and turned to meet his foe with 70,000 troops at Chicamauga Creek, Tennessee, September 1-20, 1863. Bragg broke through the line and Rosecrans was forced to retreat to Chattanooga, where Thomas took command. After weeks of bloody battle, Bragg's army was routed and driven back into Georgia. Burnside, then, finally accomplished the advance into Eastern Tennessee to relieve the Unionists there, but not until after the disaster at Chicamauga.[6]

The BEARD family arrived to play an important role in the activities of the camp, moving from Milford in 1850 to settle in the eastern part of the village. They operated a flour mill in the "Germany" section and reared five sons and four daughters: Sarah, William, Jennie, Gabriel, Charlotte, John, George, Charles and Margaret (Birdie). They also reared a granddaughter who was the daughter of Charlotte Snyder.

When war was declared, Mr. Beard built a brick house opposite the railroad station (Illus. No. 49, No. 105) where he boarded army officers. After the war, he sold the building to William Knicely who kept a grocery there for many years.

"Mother Beard" helped the village doctor, Dr. Buckingham, nurse the sick and wounded in the "Old 70 Barracks Hospital." She also wrote letters home for them and was in many ways a great comforter.

The Beard house burned after 1865 and then Mr. Beard bought the Heaton house (Illus. No. 49, No. 83) by the public school. About this time he opened a blacksmith's and wagon maker's shop near the site of his ruined home and worked at these trades until he passed away. All of his children eventually married and had homes of their own. There are twelve grandchildren and many great-grandchildren of the Beards, many of whom live in Cincinnati. The granddaughter they raised, Mrs. Edw. S. Begler, also lives in Cincinnati.

During the war, Presdent Lincoln and his close associates visited the encampment and were guests of the Beards. The youngest daughter of the family was given the nickname "Birdie" by the President; she married Ambrose (Dick)

Alspach who had a blacksmith shop in Miamiville for forty-five years.[7] They had a daughter Ethel.

William H. Queal was agent for the Pennsylvania Railroad during the war, as he worked for that company for thirty-six years.

Our chapter on church history reveals that church services were not held for non-military congregations in Camp Dennison during the time it was a Union camp. Members apparently attended church in the neighboring villages, if, indeed, they did not move there for the duration of the war.

The Zumstein farm was located at the end of the lane bearing that name. John Zumstein bought the sutler rights at the camp during the war, paying 10 cents for each soldier on the grounds. He had the sole rights to sell supplies to the soldiers, and the buildings where he conducted his business were located along the railroad track just south of Building No. 11 (Illus. 49). They had one son Frank who established the Cincinnati Program and Publishing Co. He married Jessie Warman of Cincinnati and they had one daughter, Edna, who married Lawrence Herschede.[8] For many years the Zumstein home was used as a summer residence only and was sold to the Ohio Gravel Co. about 1952. One of the sheds on the Zumstein farm looked, in its younger days, very much like the military post office, complete with a post window in one outer wall. It must have been moved to the farm after the Civil War.

AS FOR THE DISMANTLING OF THE CAMP

Mrs. Jessie F. Lytle testifies in a letter written to us July 3, 1954, that "The Buckingham farm and the Price farm were leased by the government, and they beautified it considerably by setting out poplar trees where there were none, etc., for of course many of the forest trees were long cut down to make way for farming.

"After the war closed, Nimrod Price allotted his farm land with some exceptions and the town of Camp Dennison came into being.

"Most of the houses were made of reconstructed barracks. I could name them all to you up and down the roads. The house you live in (140) was the house of Mahlon Price, son of Nimrod. The house next door (139) was the house of Brown (Marius Price), the next one was the house of Mark Price (138). The Mills family used to live there. The Sam Drake house was the house of Martha Price Leever (154). The one where Mrs. Cochran lived was the home of John Price (148). Milton Price's house stood between her house and the Glazier house (149), and was moved down and is the house my father had and where he died (115). All these houses and others besides were mostly made of barracks. But not the Fry house (110) or the one next door (111) or the Ruff house (125) or Marcia Lucia's house (136); they were built by a man named Browneyes and his partner whose name I do not remember."[9]

The Secrest Monument

Here is a contemporary account of the erecting of the granite monument on State Route 126, at the southern end of the village. The marker stands on a triangular plot of ground carefully maintained by the county roads department as a tiny park.

Secrest Monument in 1932 at time of dedication.

"Some headway has been made in appropriately marking with bronze tablets the historic spots in Cincinnati and vicinity so that future generations can have some comprehension of their significance.

"The most ambitious attempt in this line was the erection of the monument which recites in durable bronze and granite the great military achievements that were wrought at Camp Dennison.

"The monument is situated at the intersection of the Glendale-Milford Pike and Kugler Mill Road. The idea of a monument originated with Jacob Secrest, of Cincinnati, former commander of the Department of Ohio, G.A.R., and former senior vice commander-in-chief of the national organization which is now slowly fading into the mists of memory.

"In October, 1930, Mr. Secrest was one of the guests at a homecoming of veterans at the historic camp site and that same month at a dinner given in his honor in Memorial Hall he suggested that the Grand Army and its allied organizations create a fund for the purpose. Mr. Secrest set the example by soliciting and acquiring contributions of money.

"The members of the committee in charge were in addition to Mr. Secrest: Attorney Michael Heintz, Judge Simon Ross, Mathias W. Kugler (certainly not Mathias born in 1780, or his son Mathias born in 1821), Mrs. Anna M. Allen of the Women's Relief Corps, Mrs. Ethel Chambers and James M. Hughes. Mrs. Allen was president of the committee, Mrs. Chambers, secretary, and Mr. Hughes, treasurer. The money for the erection of the monument was contributed by the following organizations and relatives of some of the men who trained for war while in that camp: Women's Relief Corps, Ladies of the G.A.R., Sons and Daughters of Veterans, the Auxiliary of the S. of V., Women's Relief Corps of Milford, O., the husband of the president of the latter body, Mrs. Mary E. Thomas, having been encamped there.

[A flagpole was donated by Marcia Lucia Buckingham at this time but later rusted and had to be removed.]

"The plot of ground was donated by the Pennsylvania Railroad Company and Mr. and Mrs. Henry M. Pinkvoss. On a beautiful Indian summer day, October 2, 1932, the monument was unveiled in the presence of a throng of spectators. Waving fields of corn and wheat now cover the territory where, in the sixties, thousands of young men received their training for grim battle on distant fronts. The bronze tablet on the face of the monument contains the list of organizations that were either mustered in or mustered out at the famous camp. A perusal of them plainly shows the scope of this training center. They follow:

"First Three Months' Service. April, 1861. (Period of enlistment were of short duration while it was believed that the war would not last long.)

Infantry—Fourth, Fifth, Sixth, Seventh, Eighth, Ninth, Tenth, Eleventh, Twelfth.

Infantry, Three years, Dennison Guards—Fourth Independent Company Sharpshooters, Eighth Independent Company Sharpshooters.

Second O.V.I., Third O.V.I., Fourth O.V.I., Fifth O.V.I., Sixth O.V.I., Eighth O.V.I., Ninth O.V.I., Tenth O.V.I., Eleventh O.V.I., Twelfth O.V.I., Thirteenth O.V.I., Seventeenth O.V.I., Twenty-eighth O.V.I., Thirty-fourth O.V.I., Thirty-ninth O.V.I., Forty-seventh O.V.I., Fiftieth O.V.I., Fifty-second O.V.I., Fifty-fourth O.V.I., Fifty-seventh O.V.I., Seventieth O.V.I., Seventy-ninth O.V.I., Eighty-third O.V.I., Eighty-ninth O.V.I., 106th O.V.I., 108th O.V.I.

Cavalry. Three years—Fourth, Fifth, Ninth, Eleventh, Third Independent Company, Sixth Independent Company.

Ohio Artillery. Three years—Second Regiment Heavy Artillery, First Ohio Volunteer Light Artillery.

Independent Battery, Three years—Fifth Independent Battery Light Artillery, Eighth Independent Battery Light Artillery, Tenth Independent Battery Light Artillery, Fourteenth Independent Battery Light Artillery, Eigtheenth Independent Battery Light Artillery, Twenty-first Independent Battery Light Artillery, Twenty-fourth Independent Light Artillery.

Brigade Bands, three years—Third Brigade, Third Division, Fourth Army Corps.

Infantry, one year—175th, 181st, 183rd.

Cavalry, six months—Fourth Independent Battalion.

One Hundred Days Service, Infantry, 1864—137th, 138th, 139th, 146th, 147th, 149th, 152nd, 153rd, 154th, 155th, 156th, 165th, 168th.

"The tablet is not far distant from the Waldsmith house, a brick structure erected in 1806.[10]"

1. See Genealogy Table.
2. Newspaper Clippings on Cincinnati, Cincinnati Public Library, Vol. II, p. 176.
3. Other state militia encampments in Hamilton County were Camp Harrison, situated on the site of Chester Park; Camp Clay, which was on the large plot of ground where the gas works in the East End stand; Camp John McLean, named for Justice John McLean; Camp Corwine, named for Major Richard M. Corwine; Camp Colerain was north of the city.
4. *History of Clermont Co.*, Rockey and Bancroft.
5. *History of Clermont Co.*, Rockey and Bancroft (pp 239-242).
6. *Abraham Lincoln*, by Lord Chesterfield, Garden City Publishing Co., Garden City, N. Y., 1917, pp. 342-360.
7. Letter from Ruth B. Armstrong, c/o 700 Main St., Cincinnati, Ohio
8. *Memoirs of the Miami Valley*, Vol. III, Biographical.
9. Letter from Mrs. Jessie Price Lytle, St. Petersburg, Florida.
10. Clipping from Cincinnati paper. Correction—the Waldsmith home is made of stone, not brick, and date of erection was 1804, not 1806.

Chapter IV

GRAND VALLEY 1865-1917

" . . . *There is at present a small village of some twenty-five buildings, including a church, a tavern, a store, a few smaller shops and the railroad station. The houses are generally surrounded by little gardens, and round about the grain fields flourish. On the whole it is a quiet little spot, and on the roads — as yet unpaved — one hardly meets a soul.*"

. . . . H. A. Ratterman, 1870
"*Germany, Die Erste Deutsche Niederlassung in Miamithale.*"

This chapter takes its title from the attempted name change in the early 1870's. Persons feeling that "Camp Dennison" was unworthy of the setting succeeded in having the post office address changed to "Grand Valley, Ohio." However, the railroad refused to accept the new name on its timetables so that the resulting confusion had to be ended by a return to the military name which had been used until the present.

After the closing of the camp, the farms which had been leased by the government were restored to their original (and now prosperous, if we are to believe the charges of the "exhorbitant rates") owners. Poplar trees had been set out to mark the lanes in the middle of the camp. Nelle Falgner tells that when her family bought the Haffenbradl farm in 1921, she inquired of her father about the profusion of asters in the fields. She was told that when the Union soldiers had nothing better to do, they busied themselves planting flowers.

A land development program was begun not because of a housing shortage in Camp Dennison, but to accommodate the new commuting class. As more people not directly engaged in agriculture began to make their homes here, they rode the trains to Cincinnati or points north, as for example to Kings Mills or Loveland. The schedules called for regular and frequent stops of trains at the ticket office on Lincoln Road.

At this time some men envisaged rows of large homes surrounded by noble trees and tufty lawns supplanting the stubble of neglected fields and a few hardened hoofprints of a ghostly cavalry. Nimrod Price, heir to the holdings of Daniel Price, sold his farm to speculators and the town of Camp Dennison came into being.[1]

MUNSON's subdivision extended roughly from Zumstein Lane on the north to Lincoln Road on the south, separated from the Montauk Road by a narrow strip belonging to Charles Beard. Mr. Beard also owned from Montauk on the east to an alley on the west, south to Campbell Avenue and north to Locust.

Otto PALM had acreage bordered by Cunningham Road, Pinkvoss Lane, Price Street and the BRAUNEIS-HERMAN lot, which was from Kilgore east to Palm's on the west, and running north and south between Cunningham Road and Pinkvoss Lane. The DENNISON VILLAGE ADDITION was a strip of land along the southern side of Lincoln Road east of Montauk.[2]

Mr. Leonidas Tittle, a carpenter, came to Camp Dennison to help Munson construct the houses. Before progress could continue, however, mistakes in the survey had to be corrected and a number of lots were re-purchased. The Tittles lived in the house built by Charles Beard while Mr. Tittle built a home on the foundation of Daniel Price's second residence, but it burned to the ground before it was completed. The undaunted Mr. Tittle, father of three, set to work and raised another frame immediately. This foundation then has supported three buildings, an enviable record for any pile of stones. In the basement the wall supporting the fireplace is nearly three feet thick.

The burning of the Tittle house points its tragic finger to a little appreciated fact about country living: that pumps and

Dr. Buckingham's House on Washington St. Now owned by Mrs. Fern Dunn. On Illustration this is No. 136.   Photo by Rob Paris.

wells were the only source of water. Some were public, as was the one below the cemetery hill, and others were on private property, as on Knicely's place, or Fry's. These wells are now capped but presumably still contain water. Water for every household need was carried by hand and in case of fire there were scarcely enough people to form a "bucket line." Queal's on Lincoln Road, Green's and Longley's on Camp, Williams' on Zumstein . . . all these houses burned to the ground. Many a frightened householder, trying to save furniture, simply threw or carried articles just outside the doors where they were blistered and burned beyond recognition by sparks.

Munson died before realizing his glorious suburbia. However, a few large houses, with noble trees and aged lawns, did germinate in this era of overenthusiastic land development. On our map of houses, they are numbered: 51, 83, 84, 110, 111

Dr. Alfred Buckingham
    Mrs. Edna Van Pelt Buckingham, wife of Dr. Buckingham.
        Miss Marcia Lucie Buckingham, daughter of Dr. Buckingham.

and 136. I am sure the cliff dwellers of our modern cities find a measure of tranquility in these buildings whose main lines lead toward the sky, rather than promoting a left-right jerking motion and squinting necessary to delineate the fashionable homes of today.

Camp Dennison Building Association

Records for the years 1885-1886 exist with mention of activity in 1880. John Zumstein, the president, attended meetings infrequently; W. B. Knicely was vice president. The Building Association was a money lending agency.[3]

An old book of township maps reveals a charming "Business Directory of Camp Dennison" around 1870:[4]

  "W. H. Queal   R. R. Station Agent
    G. A. Simpson Dry Goods
    W. B. Knicely   Plasterer
    S. S. Vosburg   Carpenter
    Wm. Beard   Blacksmith and Justice of the Peace."

In addition to these there were the Eberhardt Bulldog Kennels established in 1836 and the Fischer Yeast Company founded in 1891.

The Granite Improvement Company

This company excavated southeast of the Secrest Monument. The Pennsylvania Railroad used the earth for rail beds at the Undercliff Yards below Linwood.

The Post Office

The Post Office was at one time in the railroad depot, then was moved across the tracks to Clement Street (House No. 95, Illus. 49), then was transferred to Cunningham Road (House No. 84), and was then moved back to Clement Street to the house of Mrs. Edsall. Its final journey was to the main street after Ed Leiman became postmaster, and remains here unto the present day.

The Taverns

Baumheckel's saloon was housed in the building now used as the Miami Valley Inn, a large building at Ulrich Street on the main route.

Another tavern (at the southeast corner of the main street and Lincoln Road) was owned by the Mr. Tittle mentioned above. His manager evidently made more profits from the business than the owner, and the business soon shut down.

The General Store

was first in the building on the southwest corner of Lincoln and Route 126 where Mr. Hathman now lives. Ed McAfee bought it from Bill Cordes, who later committed suicide. Mr.

Early picture of grocery store with Howard Brown and Frank Hodges.

McAfee removed his business to the building it now occupies, and in 1905 sold it to William J. Brown and Son (in reality the son, who was not yet twenty-one). Mr. Brown and his brother ran a general store which sold everything from food to felt boots; he would walk from house to house taking orders, then deliver them by wagon. He in turn sold the store to Edward Leiman in 1911. The Browns opened a store in Cincinnati which they operated many years.[5]

The Library

After the Cincinnati Library became the library for all of Hamilton County in 1896, a branch was established on Lincoln Road in the building in back of No. 11. Col. Metcalfe was in charge. Mrs. Edsall later kept the library in her own home on Clement Street.

Telephone Service

The Citizens' Telephone Company of Clermont County, Ohio, operated exchanges and furnished some telephone service in the towns of Batavia, New Richmond, Loveland, Milford, Tobasco, Edenton, Goshen and New Boston prior to 1910. Then their plant and equipment were purchased by the Cincinnati and Suburban Bell Teleponhe Company.

In Milford, Ohio, an exchange was opened by the City and Suburban Telephone Association (forerunner of the present Cincinnati and Suburban Bell Telephone Company) on November 6, 1902, at Garfield and High Streets. It served eight subscribers in Milford proper.

By November, 1903, lines had been extended across the river to stations on Plainfield Pike in Hamilton County. In the early part of 1904 the lines were extended along Route 126 to Camp Dennison, connecting the telephones in the saloon of Frank Baumheckel and the residences of Jennie Queal and John Zumstein. These are the first known subscribers to telephone service in Camp Dennison.[6]

Mt. Olivet Baptist Church

The Mt. Olivet Baptist Church was established May 5, 1888, by the Negro citizens of the community. Some of the first members were: George, Eliza, Louis, William, Lucius, Susie, Rachel, Hattie and Fannie Walton, Harry Matthews, Harry, Cynthia and Nancy Teaman (Tieman), Samuel and Etta Fox, Andrew and Alice Talley, Charles Worsham, Charles A. and Thomas Jones, Nellie and Carrie Prather, Minnie Bennett, Newton Brown, Silas Gilard, John Boston, Nannie Owens, Daisy Cisco, Blanche Steward and Florie Campbell. The first church which was built "below the hill" on the north side of House No. 8 burned in 1894 or 1895, and a larger church, erected on Campbell Street in 1896, has been used by Negro congregations until the present. Mr. George Walton mortgaged his home in order to help pay for the erection of the present church. The following is a partial list of ministers who have served this church: W. W. Smith, W. A. Chambers, Louis Burr, Mr. Simpson, Charles Jones, B. D. Scott, R. H. Walker, W. P. Chapman, William Frazier, Earl Jones, Mr. Burgess, James Allen, Rufus Turner, S. A. Brown. The Reverend Mr. R. Fincher is the present pastor.[7]

Mt. Olivet Baptist Church, 1956.

The following families moved into our village during the period of 1863 to 1917 and have been supporters of the Mt. Olivet Baptist Church.

George WALTON, albeit a generous man, had grown tired of donating his free services to southern plantation owners, and had joined the Union army as a cook. At the war's end he found himself in Camp Dennison where he remained and reared his children: Louis, Alice, Etta, Susan, Rachel, Eugene, Hattie, William, Lucius and Ralph. The others died in infancy. Louis for many years was Superintendent of the Orphanage in Avondale, Cincinnati, Ohio, and was highly regarded by everyone with whom he came into contact. He and his wife Fannie had five children: (1) Harold married Lula Gordon, lives in San Francisco and has two daughters, Frances Pitts and Lela Deane; (2) Morris, having spent most of his time teaching and counseling youth, is vice president of McCall Industrial School in Cincinnati, and since his retirement from actual teaching owns and operates the Sohio Filling Station on Route 126, which service station his father and mother had built in 1932; (3) Harriette (Lyda) Henderson is dietitian and does some catering. She has one daughter who is a social service worker in New York City. (4) Louis G. is deceased, and (5) Lena Boyd has a son George and a daughter Peggy. The second child of George Walton was Alice who married Andrew Talley and who had one son, Roscoe. The third child was Etta, the wife of Samuel Fox. They lived for many years in House No. 12, Illus. 49, and had four children, Ray, Anna, Leroy and Alice. The fourth child was Susan Dent. Fifth was Rachel whose first husband was Stewart Jones and whose sons were Earl, who still lives in Camp Dennison in House No. 91, Illus. 49, and George who lives in Cincinnati. Rachel married secondly George Prather and their daughter Medell lives with her father next door to the Mt. Olivet Baptist Church. The sixth child, Eugene, married Clara Worsham and had two children, Eugene and Geneva. Seventh was Hattie Fletcher who had one son Virgil, and eighth was William whose daughter Ariel Drake is married to a minister in Chicago.[8]

William WORSHAM came here as a boy with his family from Ripley, Ohio, probably around 1880. In the early 1900's he married Zella Tucker. Their family consisted of Gladys Mundy, Cincinnati, Ohio, who has one daughter; Charles who has three sons; Alfred, Walter and Philip who live on Camargo Pike out of Miamiville, Ohio: William, San Francisco; Florence Cooper, New York City; and Lena and Paul who are deceased. Philip has four children.[9]

One of the oldest residents of our village is Bill CISCO, whose father, Crawford Cisco, came to this part of the country prior to the Civil War. During the war he worked for the Zumstein family. Following the war he married Liza Martin and they had four children, two of whom died young. Bill has lived here all of his life and for the past few years, his sister, Georgia Findlay, has also lived here. Bill says that his father came from Oklahoma and that he is a full blooded Cherokee Indian. Morris Cisco, a brother of Crawford, also lived here and his son, Charles (Tompie), lived here until his death. Lucy, the widow of Charles, is now in the Home for the Aged in Cincinnati.[10]

Esther Cisco BROADUS was born in Camp Dennison and lived here with her aunt, Birdie Cross, on Ulrich Street until she moved to Cleveland, Ohio prior to the First World War. She later married Marshall Broadus and in 1938 they moved back to our village where they bought House No. 53 (Illus 49). Mr. Broadus died in July 1955.[11]

Robert BENNETT and his family moved here about 1912. Six of their children lived here as children: Ferguson and Robert who are not living; Bill who has one daughter and lives in Madisonville, Cincinnati, O.; Henry who lives in New York; Mary, whose daughter, Patsy Grant, lives in Hamilton and who has three children; and Hester who is married to John Ferguson and lives in House No. 95 (Illus. 49). Hester and John have four children, Charles who lives in Cincinnati, Philip who is attending Central State College at Wilberforce, Ohio, Nancie and Elaine who are still in school at Indian Hill. Another daughter of Mr. and Mrs. Robert Bennett is Leontine Hathman who with her husband and son lives in House No. 15 (Illus. 49).[12]

Eliza and William DAVIS came here in the early 1900's. For many years they were employed at the Miami Boat Club in Miamiville, Ohio, and Liza's culinary skill is very well known. William died in 1940. Mrs. Davis still lives in her home on Campbell St. (House No. 56, Illus. 49)[13]

William FRAZIER and his family also came here in the early 1900's. Mrs. Frazier and two of the daughters, Ruby and Thelma, are now deceased. The other children are as follows: Joseph lives in Loveland; James in Cincinnati and has one child; Dorothy Stancil, who graduated from Ohio State University, was a WAC during World War II, and a former teacher, lives in Philadelphia; Bessie Richmond lives in Boston; Elsie lives in Cincinnati; and Mary Alice and Richard live here in their house on the corner of Lincoln and Route 126 (House No. 51, Illus. 49).[14]

BIOGRAPHICAL SKETCHES

The following sketches are of the families inhabiting Camp Dennison between 1863 and 1917. Some are notable as proprietors of businesses. Others lent their names to our streets (now paved). A few led lives of public service.

Dr. ABBOTT was a colleague of Dr. Buckingham's in the post-Civil War days, around 1888. He lived where Morris Walton now lives (No. 99, Illus. 49).[15]

Mr. and Mrs. William ALLEN had a dairy at the corner of Kugler Mill and Camp Roads . . . and Camp Road was for years called "Allen Road" from Kugler Mill to Lincoln, and Price Street the rest of its length. They did not have any children but reared Josephine Linville who is married and living in Oroville, California. Mr. Allen was Methodist Sunday School Superintendent from 1897 to 1908, before moving to Franklin, Ohio; Mrs. Allen played the church organ and taught Sunday School.[16]

David and John ANDERSON came here as young men and worked on the Peckenpaugh farm. Another brother, Charles, was in the Navy and did not live here until his later life, when after a few years he died. David married Dora Gash from Milford in 1907 and they lived for years in the house on the corner of Camp and Cunningham Roads where Elva lives at the present time. (Illus. 49, No. 137). They had six children: Caroline is married to Frank Reindel and lives in Cincinnati. They had one adopted child who was accidentally killed when he was nine. Charles is married to Amanda Harper and lives in Mason, Ohio; they have two boys. Mildred is married to George Bowen and lives in Madisonville, Cincinnati, Ohio;

Back Row: Mrs. Wm. B. Knicely, Lillie Buckingham Robinson. Ella Ruff. Mrs. Nettie Webber, Mrs. Emma Little.
Front Row: Mrs. William Mills, Mrs. Harriet Tittle, Mrs. Agnes Marsh. Mrs. Alice Ruff, Mrs. Gossman.   About 1890.

they have two girls and one boy. Lawrence is in the service and is married to Marian Maphet. Elva is married to Harold (Boots) Maphet and lives in the Anderson home; she has one boy and two girls. Elva is active in the Primary Department of the Sunday School. Jean is married to Marlin Patton, has one boy, and lives in Mt. Sterling, Ohio.[17]

John Anderson married Edith McAllister from Camp Dennison. The McAllisters lived in one of the houses below the Knicely property along the railroad track, houses which have been torn down. They had three children. Edward is married to Evelyn Stevens and has six children. Permelia is married to Jess Anderson (Buck) from Miamiville and had four children: Marjory, John Edward, Raymond who was drowned in the

Little Miami River a few years ago, and Cindy. Permelia and Jess perform a very necessary and appreciated service for the village, collecting waste. Marjory Dunn is divorced from her husband and lives with her mother in the old John Anderson home on Clement St. (Illus. 49, No. 93). She has two daughters Irene and Georganne.[18]

Joseph M. and Amy BARRERE lived on the Quayle farm for approximately 15 years following 1913, after which they moved to Milford, Ohio, where Mr. Barrere later became Mayor. Mrs. Barrere died in 1917. They had six children: Harold, who is married to Mabel Prather and has one daughter, Ruth; (shortly after their marriage they lived on the Pinkvoss property in Camp Dennison, and Mabel's two children by a former marriage, Marie and Robert McCammon, went to school here); Gerald (Gary) and Dorothy Barrere have one daughter Wilma; Roy and Mary have a son Miles; Donna is married to Harry Eveland and lives in Terrace Park, Ohio — they have two sons, Clarence and George, both of whom are married; Arnold (Tom) and

Norman Little, Rolf Pinkvoss, Johnny Walsh, Henry Pinkvoss and Duff Boles in front of Knicely's Store. About 1916.

Mary also live in Terrace Park and have one son Billy living, their other son, Thomas, having been killed in an automobile accident in 1954; Mary Barrere is married to Marcellus Chandler and lives in Milford — their two children, both married, are Donald and Amy.[19]

John and Elizabeth Casper BAUER moved here about 1907. (Their house is No. 7, Illus. 49). Bill Bauer married Josephine Walters and had three boys and a girl, and lived on the Queal-Gant farm. Two of his children, Bertha and John, died of diphtheria within two days in 1922. His other sons, Wilbur and

Charles, went to school in Camp Dennison. Wilbur died in recent years.

Charles Bauer's first wife was Rose Wolfer and they had four boys and three girls. He is now married to Josephine Benken, who is also a former resident of Camp Dennison.

George Bauer is married to Irma Wulfeck. Velma Bauer is married to Ray Specker and lives in Terrace Park, Ohio. They have two sons, John Raymond who owns a drug store in Dayton, Ohio, and Robert Winton who is an officer in the army. Velma and Ray have five grandchildren.

Mrs. Elizabeth Bauer died in her daughter Velma's home in her 72nd year. Mr. John Bauer died in 1932.[20]

Mr. and Mrs. August (Gus) BENKEN came to Camp Dennison in 1909 to take care of the dairy for Mr. Pinkvoss. They first lived in the frame house between the two stone houses and in 1915 lived in the Waldsmith home. They moved to Milford in 1927 and Mr. Benken died there in 1928. Mrs. Benken died in March 1956. They had eight children: William is married to Helen Haley and had one daughter; they live in Milford. Bernard (Bernie) is married to Grace Oligee, lives in

Telegraph Station on Pennsylvania Railroad, early 1900's.
Chester Bodley in door.

Milford and has six children; their daughter Laura is married to James Miller and lives in Camp Dennison. Josephine is married to Charles Bauer. August (Gus) lives in Bellevue, Kentucky; he is married to Matilda Schmidt and has one boy and one girl. Edward is married to Evelyn Motz and lives in Newtown, Ohio; they have nine children — six girls and three boys; three of Edward's daughters have become nuns and are teachers. Edna is married to George Motz and lives in Terrace Park;

they have twelve children — seven boys and five girls; her oldest daughter is also a nun. John is married to Virginia Meyer, who lived in Camp Dennison with her mother, father and sister Rita; they have four girls and one boy and have a greenhouse in Wyoming, Ohio. Herman is married to Marie Cook and has three boys; he owns the Lockland Florist Shop, Lockland, Ohio.[21]

Conrad BROWN came to Camp Dennison about 1868. He was a cooper, and before coming here he worked on the Cincinnati-Covington Suspension Bridge. The house they lived in (Illus. 49, No. 113) is composed of two sections. The southern half was moved from the "Germany" section, and to this Mr. Brown built another wing. At one time the southern half was a bakery, and in the wall of the basement there is still an oven. A saloon was kept on the north side. After Mrs. Rosina Brown died, Mr. Brown married Theresa Steidle Southworth who had a daughter Sarah. Conrad Brown died in 1898. (See Wartnaby).[22]

Mr. and Mrs. Chrif BRUNNER and their family settled on the Allen farm on Camp Road in 1907, and lived there until approximately 1926. They had six children: Elsie, who is now deceased, married Joe Mintkenbaugh; Mabel is married to Howard Brooks and lives in Indian Hill, Ohio — they have two boys and one girl; Cora is married to Eli Cox and lives on Shawnee Run Road near Milford — they have a boy and a girl; Charles who died in 1956 was married to Nellie Pucket and lived on Eight Mile Road in Anderson Township, Hamilton Co., Ohio — they have four boys and two girls; Clarence is married to Mary Florey, has two boys and one girl, and lives in Terrace Park; Bryan is married to Ruth Peckenpaugh and has one son. Clarence operates the Cities Service Gasoline Station in Terrace Park.[23]

Alfred BRYANT worked for the Pennsylvania Railroad and moved to Camp Dennison with his wife Ella about 1890. Their house was on the west side of the road near the Miamiville bridge, but they moved to Miamiville when the 1913 flood ruined their home. Two of their daughters, Margaret Hooler and Clara Timpe are deceased. The other daughter, Rose, is married to James Holmes and lives in Loveland, Ohio. She has five daughters, all married. William Bryant, who is married to Elsie Applegate, had two sons and two daughters but lost one son in World War II. Arthur is married to Laura Hessler and has seven living children. Both William and Arthur live in Loveland. Clara Timpe had one daughter and one son.[24]

The BUSH family lived in Dr. Buckingham's house on Washington Street. There were five children, Fred, Mara, Mamie, Eddie and Hattie, as shown by the Sunday School records of

1870. Mrs. Bush was a good friend of Dr. Buckingham's wife, and it was when they moved that Dr. Buckingham bought this house (Illus. 49, No. 236).

Mr. and Mrs. Charles BOYD moved here about 1912. After living on the Paxton farm and the Allen farm, they moved to Cunningham Road (No. 150). Mr. Boyd's mother, who lived with them prior to her death, was born and raised on Indian Hill, Ohio, and attended church and school in our village prior to the Civil War. Mr. Boyd's father was inducted into the Union Army in Camp Dennison. Mr. and Mrs. Boyd had two children: Clifford married Eva Rahn and, after her death, married Mary Graves McShane. He and Mary had one daughter. Clifford's sister Edna is married to Ed Howard and lives in Columbus, Ohio. Their son Jack died while a small boy. Their son Robert is now a minister in Columbus[25]

Frank BAUMHECKEL owned and operated the saloon on Route 126 off and on from 1902 to 1928. From 1917 to 1920 he ran a service station. He is now 86 years of age and is a patient in Drake Memorial Hospital, Cincinnati, Ohio.[26]

Mr. and Mrs. Henry BORGERDING bought the Beard house on Cunningham Road in 1915. Mr. Borgerding and Mr. Schwey (Mrs. Borgerding's father who lived with them) died within a couple of days of each other in 1918 during the flu epidemic and they had a double funeral. Mrs. Borgerding's sister, Emma Schwey, also lived there until her marriage in 1927 to Mr. Goerig, after which she moved to Woodlawn, Washington. In 1933 Mrs. Borgerding also went to Woodlawn and died there the following year.

Helen Schwey CARTER, a daughter of Mrs. Borgerding's brother, moved here in 1944 with her husband, Harry, when they bought House No. 147 on Daniel Street. They have one son, Harry Francis, who lives at home. Helen's mother, Mrs. Rose Schwey, and her brother, George Schwey, also live with them.[27]

When Mr. and Mrs. George CASE came here with their granddaughters, Gertrude and Emily Case, they first lived on the Peckenpaugh farm on Cunningham Road. They later moved to a location across from the village grocery on the highway, into a house which has been removed. Mr. Case was struck and killed by an automobile as he walked home from Milford one night in 1922. Mrs. Case died some years later after she had left Camp Dennison. Gertrude is married to Norman Little. Emily's first husband was Joseph Lello and they had one son. After Mr. Lello's death she married Russell Ferguson who died in 1955. She lives in Fairfax, Ohio.[28]

At one time two COCHRAN brothers lived here. Charles came with his wife Eva Blackburn and family in 1889. His wife's father, James Blackburn, and brother, Willis, lived here prior to that time. Mr. and Mrs. Charles Cochran had nine children: Dart who is married to Eminence Morris, has two children and lives in Blue Ash, Ohio; Jim who died during World War I with flu; Florence who was married to Clinton DeMar of Maderia, Ohio and who is not now living; Arch who is married to Ruby Fullen and had three children, two of whom are living, and who lives in College Hill, Cincinnati; Mary who is the widow of Clint Smith and lives in House No. 66 (Illus. 49); Chris who lives in Blanchester, Ohio, is married to Lenora Davis and who has six children; Eva who was married to Amos Wells, has four children and who lives in the old home; and Hilda who died in 1925 in her 17th year. Three of Eva's children are also living in Camp Dennison now: Dorothy McQuiddy, Evelyn Drusell, and Lawrence. Both Charles and his wife died in 1933. Mrs. Cochran was killed at the railroad crossing by the old Queal farm on Route 126 between here and Milford.[29]

Fred Cochran and his wife Eva came here in 1914 or 1915. Mrs. Cochran when widowed continued to live in their home (House No. 148, Illus. 49) until her death in 1953. They had two of their several children with them when they lived here: Zella married Clarence Woodruff and died in her early twenties. Hazel died while still very young.

The COMPTON house was the building which is now the Miami Valley Inn on Route 126 (No. 63, Illus. 49). This property was purchased by Rebecca Compton from William and Eliza Beard in 1869. A younger Compton family, Mr. and Mrs. Frank Compton, lived in House 85 (Illus. 49). Their three children were Oren, Lillian and Theresa. Gladys Compton, Frank's sister, was secretary of the Sunday School in 1884. Oren's son, Oren Jr. now lives in Norwood, Ohio.[30]

Henry CORDES and his family came to Camp Dennison about 1887. He maintained a grocery where Hathmans live (House No. 15, Illus. 49). They had eight children: Fanny, Emma, Ida, Charles, Will, Harry, Anna and Clara. Anna died in infancy. After the death of his first wife, Mr. Cordes married a Mrs. St. John. Will Cordes married Florence Adamson (a sister of Mrs. Bert Jackson) and they had three children: Floyd, who is remembered around town as a boy when he lived with Mrs. Edsall, and who now lives in New York; Herman, who died of spinal meningitis; and a baby girl who died at birth. Mrs. Cordes died during childbirth. Will Cordes some years later took his own life.[31]

Clara Cordes was an active Methodist and sang in the church choir. She married William Winkelman and had one daughter who is not living. Mrs. Winkelman has three grandchildren and nine great-grandchildren.

Addie Drake, who was a sister of Sam Drake, was married

to George CULLOM. They lived in the cottage back of House No. 11 (Illus. 49) on Lincoln Road, then later moved to House No. 54. They had one daughter, Fannie, who now lives in Oroville, California. Her first husband was Ed Lewis and they had two children, Lloyd and Alice. Lloyd is now married to Alice Green and lives in Oroville, and Alice married Ralph Bolt and had three children. She died several years ago.[32]

Samuel and Emma DRAKE lived for many years on Camp Road (House No. 154, Illus. 49). Of their four children, Pearl married Willard Rich, Lillian married a Mr. Ward, Minnie married Charles Peckenpaugh, a descendant of the early settler; Mr. and Mrs. Drake's only son, Charles, was killed in a hunting accident while still a young man. After Lillian's death, her daughter, Edna, lived with her grandparents until she died at the age of six in May, 1917.[33]

Charles and Lillie DAUGHTERS lived in the Waldsmith home for three or four years prior to 1911, while they worked on the Pinkvoss farm. They had five children: Effie who lives in Milford; Charles who is married to Dorothy Martin and has a son and a daughter; Irene who is married to Ralph McAfee, lives in California — both her children died; Arthur is married to Betty Clark, has two daughters and lives in Milford, Ohio.[34]

Mr. and Mrs. Arthur DOTY were the grandparents of Arthur Lewis and Howard Brown and his brothers. The Doty's lived for some years on Route 126 near the tavern. After Mr. Doty's death, Mrs. Doty married a man by the name of Topie (Taupe). In 1903 her daughter and her husband, Mr. and Mrs. William BROWN moved here from St. Louis. They had five boys, Clarence, Arch, Chester who married Fannie Edsall, Howard and William. In 1905 Howard bought the grocery store from Ed McAfee and ran it until 1911. Mrs. Taupe died at the Brown home on Lincoln Road. In 1912 the Browns moved to Cincinnati where Howard and William had a grocery. Both are now retired.[35]

Mr. William EBERHARDT came here about 1886. At his home on Camp Road (House No. 155, Illus. 49) he kept kennels of prize English bulldogs. (See Walls.)

Melissa and Laura ELLIOTT were great-granddaughters of John Elliott who settled near Remington, Ohio prior to 1800. Besides these two women, who lived in Camp Dennison until their deaths, there were their sister Mary Vesta who died in Miamiville, Ohio, in 1893, and brothers James S. who died in Camp Dennison in 1915, and Arthur who married Adaline Jenifer and lived in Kansas City, Missouri, until he returned here after retirement. Members of the Elliott family are buried in Evergreen Cemetery, Miamiville, Ohio.[36]

Mr. and Mrs. Joseph FAUL bought the Newbigging property

in 1915. Years later they sold the farm to the Ohio Gravel Company and moved to House No. 82 (Illus. 49). Mr. Faul was a trustee of the Methodist Church for many years. They have one daughter, Velma, who is married to William GANT, and a granddaughter, Sue Ellen. Their home is also on Route 126. Velma is now an officer of the Women's Society and of the Sunday School and William is a trustee of the church.[37]

August W. and Fredericka Wolf FISCHER came to Camp Dennison in 1891 from Terrace Park, Ohio. They had two children: Minnie Luthy, and Herman who married Mary Ann (Mamie) Taylor in 1903. Miss Taylor had lived with Alice and Joseph Gregg since 1896. The Fischers lived in House No. 110 (Illus. 49) on Lincoln Road and made yeast which was distributed throughout the United States. The yeast house was later inhabited by Hereward Fry's chickens but then the Frys donated it to the Methodist Church which moved it to the church ground. It is now the Community House where the Sunday School and Women's Society meet.[38]

Herman and Mamie FISCHER had two children, August William who married Vernice Britt, Nellie Lewis's grand niece, and who has five children; and Henrietta Fredericka who lives in Hillsboro, Ohio, with her second husband, Vernon H. Seaver.[38]

Samuel FORWARD is mentioned both in the church records and Sunday School records. He was a trustee of the church at the time it was moved in 1868. Hattie and Emma Forward are also mentioned as Sunday School students. They lived on the main highway where Wesley Rahn lives (House No. 3, Illus. 49). There was a Forward who had a grocery in the building back of where Brumagems live on Lincoln Road at the railroad. Whether it was Samuel or Rollin, who is buried in the Camp Dennison cemetery, is not known. The name of Rollin Forward was taken from the gravestone and sent into Robert Ripley's "Believe It or Not" and published.

Hereward and Lucinda Hutchinson FRY bought property on Lincoln Road about 1911. Hereward was the son of William H. Fry, the noted wood carver and teacher at the Cincinnati Art Academy. Mrs. Fry was the sister of Susie Buckingham. They had no children of their own but raised the niece of Mrs. Fry, Gladys Hutchinson. Mr. Fry was a trustee of the church as well as a trustee of Symmes Township for many years. He died in Camp Dennison in 1950 and is buried in Evergreen Cemetery, Miamiville, Ohio. Mrs. Fry is living with Gladys (now Mrs. E. W. James) in Florida. The Jameses have one son.[39]

Mr. and Mrs. Sylvester FRY and their two sons first lived in Camp Dennison from 1910 to 1912 in a house on Clement St. until the house burned down. They moved back to the Buckingham farm in 1922. Allan Fry is married to Ethel Falch and lives in House No. 154 (Illus. 49), property which they bought from the Benkens in 1937. They have one son, Allan Jr., who married Lucille Langford from Camp Dennison and they have one daughter and one son. Norman and Audrey Fry live in Montgomery, Ohio. They have two boys.[40]

Mrs. Margaret GLAZIER was a widow when she came to Camp Dennison in 1870 with her two children, William and Margaret, and bought the house on Daniel Street where her grandson still lives (House No. 149, Illus. 49). When her son William married, he moved to Cincinnati. He and his wife had seven children and they visited the grandmother frequently. Her daughter was born about 1870. She married Louis Adams from Milford and had two children: Louis who lives in the old home; and Frances who was married to Nick Cosby of Terrace Park. Frances and Nick had a son and a daughter who are both married and have families. They were divorced later and Frances died in the homestead several years ago. Margaret (Midge) Glazier Adams died at home in 1954.[41]

Charles A. and Mary S. GREEN moved to the village about 1885. They had nine children who were active in the Methodist church until they moved to Milford. Nat now lives in Chicago. Lila, who wed Henry Wesche of Branch Hill, Ohio, and Lizzie, the wife of Alva Rybolt, are both dead. Delia and her husband, Magee Adams, live in Milford. Ollie is married to Wright Erion, lives in Columbus, Ohio, and has five children, Lillian, Jack, Laura, Wright Jr., and Donald. Charles, president of the Sperry Gyroscope Company, resides in New York City. Alice married Lloyd Lewis, a very active member of the Methodist congregation, and they live in Oroville, California. John, who lived in Knightstown, Indiana, and Alma who lived in Oroville both died in 1955.[42]

Joseph and Sophia HAFFENBRADL came to Cincinnati from St. Joseph, Missouri, and thence to Camp Dennison about 1890 and bought a farm on the southern side of "town." The house they built for themselves is the one the Falgner family inhabited until 1956, when all the acreage was sold to investment interests. Mr. Haffenbradl, a German immigrant, operated a dairy.[43]

The Porter HANCOCK family came to Camp Dennison in 1915 when Mr. Hancock was first employed as a teacher at the public school. Mr. and Mrs. Hancock and their daughters, Minnie and Leona, were enterprising church members until the family moved to Cincinnati, after Mr. Hancock's retirement. Minnie and Leona, both graduates of Miami University, have continued teaching: Minnie is at Concord school, Indian Hill, and Leona teaches remedial reading at the Fairfax, Mariemont and Plainville schools, Hamilton County, Ohio.[44]

Mr. and Mrs. Benson HARTZELL moved here and bought the property on Kilgore St. (House No. 127, Illus. 49) some time between the end of the Civil War and 1874 when their son William was born. Mr. Hartzell came from Pennsylvania and Mrs. Fannie Hartzell's family came from Maryland. Mr. Hartzell was a typesetter on the old *Commercial Tribune,* after which he and his son published the daily *Law Bulletin and Reporter* in Cincinnati, Ohio. They later published a weekly paper in Loveland, Ohio. Mrs. and Mr. Hartzell had four children: William who is married to Clara Prell and who had one son Wallace and one daughter Lillian; Laura Huddleston who had two sons and two daughters; Anna; and Clarence. Anna died in 1940 and Laura died several years ago.[45]

Mrs. HEATON, grandmother of Fred and Lou Anna RADCLIFFE, reared the two children. She was Mrs. William Whitelock's sister. The Heatons built a home on Cunningham Road (No. 83, Illus. 49). Mr. Heaton was killed by a train, and the gravestone in the Camp Dennison cemetery bearing the name and date "Daniel Heaton, 1875" is probably his. Heaton Street runs from the main highway to Center Street. A Hannah Radcliffe is mentioned in church records and Lillie and Mary Radcliffe had parts in a school program of 1875.[46]

Frank and Adelaide HODGES came to Camp Dennison in 1890 and settled on Zumstein's farm. They had two children: Belle, who married John Sullivan in 1903 (Belle is now deceased and John lives in Georgia); and Pearl, who married Henry Youngblutt in 1902. Mr. Youngblutt died in 1942 and Mrs. Youngblutt and daughter Edith moved to White Oak, Ohio in 1946, where her younger daughter and son-in-law, Mr. and Mrs. T. P. (Pat) Coughlin, live. Mabel Youngblutt Coughlin has a stepdaughter, Annabelle, and a son Robert.[47]

Frank Hodges' second wife was Alice Beckelheimer, and their son Tom married Genevieve Jones. They lived in Camp Dennison for some years before moving to Cincinnati. Their daughter, Virginia Hodges Cunningham of Hyde Park, Cincinnati, has three children.[47]

John and Catherine KINNEY moved from Cincinnati to the village in 1870 and later moved to the Fletcher farm which they bought. Mr. Kinney was a proof reader on the *Cincinnati Commercial Tribune.* They had three sons — George, John and William, who all became newspaper men, George and John in Cincinnati, William in New York. William's son, Harry, is with the *New York Post.* John married Mildred Newton of Miamiville and they had eight children. There were two daughters: Margaret married Hall Fletcher, son of W. W. Fletcher, and

Catherine married Ennes Dawson of Loveland. She, at the age of 92, is the only surviving member of her brothers and sisters, and still lives in Loveland, Ohio. After the death of Mr. and Mrs. Kinney, the farm was bought by Hall Fletcher. Mr. Fletcher served both on the Camp Dennison School Board and the Indian Hill District School Board.[48]

Very little is known of the A. J. KIZER family. They lived in the Fry house on Lincoln (No. 100, Illus. 49) and their children were active in the Sunday School in 1870 and 1871. Among other children there was one son, Charles, who married Cora Ludlow who lived across the street in House No. 107 (Illus. 49) with her parents and brother Edward. A. J. Kizer was Justice of the Peace in Symmes Township in 1878, 1879 and 1880 and was Secretary of the Camp Dennison Building Association in 1885 although his son Charles acted as Secretary pro tem.

William B. KNICELY was born November 1, 1834. It is not known when he first moved here but he married Nancy Skinner, the daughter of Archibald and Elizabeth Stacy Skinner, on

Pennsylvania Railroad Station.

September 4, 1867. She operated a store in the frame building in the rear of the brick building which W. B. Knicely later built and used as a store. In the later store, Mrs. Knicely used to make ice cream and sell it; they also sold coal, rice, groceries and general merchandise. Mrs. Knicely died November 21, 1908, and W. B. Knicely died March 19, 1916. They had two sons — Alexander U. S. Grant Knicely and William Archibald Knicely who died in 1934, a bachelor. Alexander (Eck as everyone called him) married Edith (Ida) Rohde on April 4, 1911, and they had one son Kenneth. Kenneth and his mother are still living in the Knicely property on the corner of Lincoln and Clement St. in back of the former store which was closed in about 1943.[49]

The John LANG family lived in the house on the hill in the rear of the Adams property from 1915 to about 1922. Of the children, Earl is married to Frances Vitello and lives in Ft. Lauderdale, Florida. They have three children living, two girls and one boy. Allan and Robert live near Newtonsville, Ohio, and are not married. Catherine is married to Elbert Wood and lives at Williams Corner, Ohio.[50]

Mr. Fred LEEVER was a school teacher from 1910-1914, living on one side of the double house at Kilgore and Jackson Streets. At the time he and his wife lived here they had three children; Maynard, Eugene and Anna Louise. Dorothy, Jane, Robert, Ruth and Lloyd Richard were born later. At the time of writing, Lloyd (Dick), his wife Virginia Farley Leever, and daughters Pamela and Barbara Ann, are living on Camp Road. Dick was Sunday School Superintendent and Virginia was a teacher in the primary department of the Sunday School.[51]

Mayme and Edward LEIMAN came to Camp Dennison in 1911 when they bought the grocery store from Howard Brown. They operated the store until 1937, when it was transferred to two nephews, John Krome and Robert Lewis. The Leimans again had charge from 1940 to 1947 when Ed Leiman retired and John KROME bought the business. Mr. Krome and his wife, Marie Gadinski Krome, and two daughters, Karen and Jeannine, live in a new home on Washington Street. Mr. Leiman became postmaster in 1914 and it was then that the post office came to its present location. Mr. Leiman died by his own hand in 1950. Mrs. Leiman and her mother, Mrs. Hershle, live in the brick house south of the store, which the Leimans built in 1924.[52]

Arthur LEWIS' father William was a house painter and he and his wife Laura and their family, came here about 1895. They lived in the Beard's house (No. 83, Illus. 49) (Besides Arthur, there were Ed, whose first wife was Fannie Cullom, and Alice who married Joseph Gregg and had four offspring: Laura, Sue, Charles and Joseph.) Arthur married Nellie Tittle and lived in the Tittle homestead, raising their two children, Hazel and Richard. Hazel's first husband, Arthur Wogenstahl, died in Our Lady of Mercy Hospital after a short illness; she had three children: Allan, Carol and Elaine Wogenstahl; she is now married to Eugene ROBINSON. Richard Lewis married Beverly Flick and has one daughter, Nancy Kay.[53]

Mr. and Mrs. John LITTLE joined us about 1880. Mrs. Little's father, William Stewart, was the brother of W. B. Knicely's mother. They first lived in the building behind Knicely's store. Their two sons, Melvin and Norman, were born here. Before long, Mr. Little built a house to the south, very near the railroad (House No. 9, Illus. 49) and another child,

Hallie, was born here. Melvin wed Lizzie Fritz of Milford; both perished in the "flu" epidemic of 1918. Norman married Gertrude Case (See Case); their son, Howard, and Lois Bartz Little live in Kenwood, Ohio, with their two children.

Hallie Little married Frank Armacost and had two children, Beryl and Richard. They lived in the Little homestead until moving to Oroville, California, in 1945. Frank died in July, 1955, and Hallie still lives in Oroville with Dick. Beryl is married to Ross Ingle Greves and lives in Houston, Texas. She has one son.[54]

Shortly after the closing of the Camp here, Cyrenius LONGLEY bought the property on the north side of Kugler Mill Road extending from the railroad to Camp Road. He had been mustered in the war into the 11th Ohio at Camp Dennison and was discharged here and liked the area so well he bought the property. The Longleys had three children: Harold, Lilien and Cyrenius Jr. (Rene). Harold was organist in the church in 1869-1870 and 1874; he had one son, Cyrenius Jr. married Lou Hutchinson and had two children. Lilien Baylis had one son Willard and they moved back to Camp Dennison in 1905; she was later married to a man named Hatcher whom she divorced; Lilien and her father lived for many years in House No. 156 (Illus. 49). Willard married Bea Startzman and they lived here until they moved to Wenatchee, Washington. Mrs. Lilien Baylis Hatcher died there in 1952. Mr. and Mrs. Willard Baylis had three children, Willard Edwin Jr. who was killed in World War II, Robert Eric, and Mary Penelope Wooton who lives in Springfield, Virginia.[55]

Different members of the Charles McAFEE family have lived here several times. The family originally moved here in 1891 and lived in the old Paxton house. The house was then nearly a hundred years old. It was a log house covered by weatherboarding. There were six children. Ed was first married to Myrtle Shively and they had two children; after her death he married Nettie Brown Willing; Ed later bought the grocery store from the Cordes family and moved it to its present location. The second son was Frank who married Edith Potter who lived on the Zumstein farm; they had one son, Chester, and a daughter, Roma Brill; Chester's son, Jack, and his wife recently lived in Camp Dennison on Lincoln Road (House No. 44, Illus. 49) but have sold to Robert and Catherine Greene Burroughs. The next child was Maud who was first married to Bay Dennison and then to his cousin, Gus Dennison; she lives in Milford and has no children. Laura married George Armstrong and has two daughters and one son. Eva is married to John Cosby and lives in Florida; Eva says that she was born during the 1893 flood and Dr. Curry of Milford floated over the fence in a boat in order to get to the house. Clyde is married to Ida

Scott and also lives in Florida; they have one girl and three boys. The McAfee family moved back to Afton, Ohio, in 1894 but returned here about 1899, moving again in 1906. After a good many years, Mrs. McAfee and Eva came back here again. They built House No. 142 (Illus. 49) on Camp Road in 1922 where Mrs. McAfee died in 1934. Mr. McAfee died in 1908.[56]

Mr. James H. McGOHAN was a school teacher here in early 1900's. His brother and sister-in-law, George and Flora McGohan, lived on the Queal farm and were active in the Sunday School. Another brother and sister, Clem and Annis, lived here years later on the Buckingham farm on Cunningham Road, at the end of Camp Road. Clem was accidently injured by a shotgun while hunting in 1931.

George and Agnes MARSH lived in House No. 97 (Illus. 49) on Clement St. in the late 1800's. They had four daughters. Lela was a school teacher here and taught many of the local residents who are still living; she is now in the Methodist Home for the Aged in College Hill. Erma was also a school teacher. There were two other daughters, Lida and Elizabeth. They were active in church work and Erma played the organ. After Mr. Marsh died they moved to Milford, Ohio.[57]

While the MEYER family did not live close to the village, their children attended school in Camp Dennison and they were well known. Joseph Henry Meyer was a recruit at Camp Dennison during the War and about 1865 purchased the farm at the southwest corner of Buckingham and Cunningham Roads. His nine children were (1) Louise, who died in infancy; (2) Joseph, who married Ella Metz; (3) Henry; (4) Mary; and (5) Anne who remained single; (6) Frank who married Ida Jergens; (7) George who married Laura McGrath, and who also lived on Cunningham Road; (8) Lillie, who married Harry Buckingham of Miamiville; (9) Elizabeth who married Cliff Oliver.

Joseph and Ella Metz Meyer bought the Cunningham farm on the northeast corner of Buckingham and Cunningham Roads about 1909 and lived there until they moved to Lebanon, Ohio about 1930. Their children attended the Methodist Church and David, the youngest son, went to school here. Of Joseph's three children, Joseph Jr. is married to Ruth Cooper and lives on the farm at Lebanon; Ruth married George Whitaker and lives near Mason, Ohio; David is Regional Executive of the Boy Scouts of America for the South Central Region, is married to Marie Zeisler and has three children: David, Frank and Betty. They are living in Memphis, Tennessee.[58]

Mr. William MILLS was an engineer on the Pennsylvania Railroad and he and his wife lived in House No. 138 (Illus. 49) on Camp Road for many years. The Mills had two children —

Etta, who married a man named Knott, and Walter who also worked for the railroad.

Percy and Callie MOORE first lived in the double house at Kilgore and Jackson Streets in 1925. They moved to Goshen, Ohio in 1939, and at the present time reside in Gano, Ohio. There were seven children in the Moore family. (1) Claude Moore married Lena Bauer and with their daughter lives in Madeira, Ohio. (2) Walter Moore's first wife was Roberta Bauer (a sister of Lena). He is now married to Sybil Geihl, they have two boys and live in Price Hill, Cincinnati, O. (3) Edward is married to Lou Swigert — they have two girls and live in Hamilton, Ohio. (4) Ida Mae married Edward Pearson, has a boy, and lives in Sharonville, Ohio. (5) Howard Paul is married to Dorothy Wardwell and lives in Maud, Ohio. They have two boys and one girl. (6) Robert married Betty Miller, lives in Sharonville, and has one son.

(7) Grace Moore married Ivan Wallace PIERCE, the son of Mr. and Mrs. Charles Pierce, who moved to the village in 1926. There were four children in the Charles Pierce family, two of whom, Lillian and Wallace, lived with their parents in Camp Dennison. Lillian is now married to Bramble Cowdry, has three children, and lives in Terre Haute, Indiana; she graduated from Bethesda Hospital School of Nursing. Grace and Wallace Pierce lived in the Pierce home on Route 126 (House No. 62) until 1942 and are now living in Sharonville, Ohio, with their boy and girl.

The Moores were always popular in Camp Dennison and they took active interest in the Methodist Church. The five older children were married by the Rev. Eugene Riffle, minister of the church for 22 years, and the children of Grace, Claude and Edward were also christened in the church.[59]

Mr. Joseph MUNCHENBACH, a native of Germany, changed his name to MINTKENBAUGH when he became a citizen of this country. He built a log cabin on Galbraith Road, in what is now the village of Indian Hill. Their five progeny were Fred, John, Caroline Mintkenbaugh Peteler, Dora Mintkenbaugh Meyers, and Elizabeth Mintkenbaugh Enders. Fred married Jennie Waits from near Newtonsville, Ohio, and occupied the old home.

Fred and Jennie reared nine children. (1) Carrie who is married to William Weigel and has five children; (2) Joseph who was married to Elsie Brunner, now dead; they raised a niece, Anna Marie Brunner; (3) Anthony who is married to Mary Fath and has two children; (4) Elizabeth (Lizzie) who is married to Joe Green and has eight children; (5) Henry who is married to Eleanor Smith; (6) Jacob (Jake) who was first married to Margaret Cribbert, later married her half sister

Laura; (7) Emma who married William Seyfried and has three children; (8) Lillie who is married to Robert Schwartz, lives next to the homestead site on Galbraith Road, and has one daughter; (9) Edna who is married to Robert Nolin, and has two daughters, Juanita Curee and Colleen.[60]

Frank and Caroline Mintkenbaugh PETELER came here about 1889. Their four children were (1) Lillie who died in 1906; (2) Anna, also deceased, who married Paul Schnetzer and who had three children; (3) Elsa who married Daniel Weber, had two boys and is living in Florida; and (4) Frances who married Harry Eigher and is now living in Terrace Park. Her husband died in 1949. Mrs. Frank Peteler died in 1925 and Mr. Peteler in 1934. Daughter Frances was at one time church organist in Camp Dennison.[61]

After John Henry NELCAMP's death in 1908, his family moved to Bethel, Ohio, after having lived here since 1900. The three children were: Ruth, who married Charles E. Jeffries and lives in Covington, Kentucky, has three children and seven grandchildren; Robert, now deceased, had one son; and Hazel who wed Lorin Daugherty, lives in Bethel, and has a son and a daughter.[62]

W. P. O'HARA was well known around town, although we have not been able to gather much authentic data about him. He worked in the Cincinnati Post Office for a number of years, taught school here at one time, taught in the Sunday School in 1871, and lived here until his death in 1909. He owned a great deal of property and at some time owned the three lots which the the church bought from the Queals in 1930. It was his idea to excavate a cellar beneath the church and install the furnace, but it is believed Charles Peckenpaugh did the digging. Mr. O'Hara made some sort of salve that would cure anything, and sold it from house to house. His housekeeper was named Mrs. Buchanan. Whether he had a family, no one seems to remember. He is buried in Miamiville, Ohio.

Henry F. and Meta PINKVOSS moved to Camp Dennison from Cincinnati in 1881. In 1884, they moved from the village to the farm they had purchased just south of the village where he operated a dairy. The Pinkvosses had three children: Rolf, Henry M., and Elsa. Mrs. Pinkvoss died in 1890 and Elsa in 1894 at the age of 10. Mr. Pinkvoss' mother, Mrs. Dorothea S. Pinkvoss, lived with them and died in 1909 at the age of 89. Mr. Pinkvoss continued to live on the farm until 1919 when he sold it to Mr. Ragland. He then moved to the village proper where he died in 1921. His son, Rolf, a veterinarian for 44 years until his retirement in 1954, graduated from the now extinct Cincinnati Veterinary College (which was not affiliated with the University of Cincinnati) and married Florence Fletcher;

they have always lived in Camp Dennison. Henry M., who is with the County Engineer's office at the Hamilton County Courthouse, married Edna Sanders, who died in 1940; Henry lives in Milford. The one grandson, Henry F. Pinkvoss, Rolf's son, married Kathryn Edwards. They live near Mt. Washington, Ohio, and have two children, Richard and Joan.[63]

Mr. Pinkvoss was gifted with that German quality of mind that still amazes us with tales of his utterly unperturbable nature. His words were often so very sensible that they made already ridiculous situations positively hilarious. As one story goes, two inebriated men returning along the "Montauk Road"

Mr. Henry F. Pinkvoss and Mr. Joseph Haffenbradl.

were having a particularly difficult time traveling because a thick fog had sprung up from the river. As they passed the desolate Kugler house, Hans said to Fritz, "My G——, I can't make it home tonight. I'm going in Pinkvoss' old warehouse here where it is dry and try to sleep until daylight." Whereupon Hans staggered in and Fritz staggered on. Hans found a stairway, and was able to climb it before he toppled to the floor and fell asleep. Presently he awoke, straightened his cap, and returned to the street, where he met Mr. Pinkvoss, dressed as always with white shirt, tie, and walking stick, making his morning tour of the farm.

"Good morning," cried Hans, "I have spent the night in your vacant building, sleeping on the floor."

"Ach! How stupid!" grunted the older man in reply. "Yust yesterday I had a fine bett moved in dat upstairs, vor die hired man dat is comink today."

Theodore TELGMANN and his sister, Meta, were the nephew and niece of Mrs. Meta Pinkvoss who came to live with her in Camp Dennison after the death of their own parents. Theodore married Estella Davis and lives in Newtown. At one time he owned a large wholesale grocery in Cincinnati. Meta married Chester Bodley (of Loveland) — both are deceased. They had one son, Theodore, who lives in Tulsa, Oklahoma. He and his wife, Virginia Evans Bodley, have three daughters, Ann, Kay, and Sandra.[64]

Lillie Fischer also lived with the Pinkvoss family. She married Stanley POND — both are deceased. Her son, Walter, is married and lives in Hamilton, Ohio.[65]

Theodore RAMMLER came to live with the Pinkvoss family in 1903. He joined the church in 1904. He married Clara Reinhart. They have three children, all married: Two girls, both Sunday School teachers, one boy, who is a minister. Mr. Rammler also teaches a Sunday School class in Bromley, Kentucky.[66]

Louise Pieper came to Camp Dennison in April 1895 and made her home with Mr. Pinkvoss and his family. She married Herman SCHROEDER, now deceased, of Cincinnati. They had one son, Lawrence, and two daughters — Katherine (Sue) and Thelma.[67]

Louis PINKVOSS (a relative of Henry F. Pinkvoss) and his wife Dorothea, moved here from Cincinnati and owned a house on Lincoln Road. Their daughter, Emma, married Leo Brand, a member of the Cincinnati Symphony Orchestra. Of their two children, Leo Jr. has been a violinist with the Cincinnati orchestra more than forty years, and Emma married Gus Doll and lives in Toledo, Ohio.[68]

The building where Miss Bessie Thompson and her father lived on Lincoln Road (House No. 14, Illus. 49), was originally owned by Mr. and Mrs. William REESE who operated a little dry goods store in the house.

The ROBINSON family, parents and seven childrn, came to Ohio from Kentucky in 1880. (1) Tom was married to Annie Gaskin and they had four sons, Lloyd, Charles, Clifford and James. They lived in Milford for many years and both died there recently.

(2) Sam married Lillie Buckingham and had three offspring: Olive (who died in her teens), Julia and Edward. Julia married Carl Volkman and lives in Hyde Park, Cincinnati, Ohio. Their son Lee is married and lives in Cincinnati, and their daughter Lois lives at home and teaches in the Cincinnati schools. Edward's daughter, Jean Anne Reeves, is a music teacher in the Cincinnati public schools.

(3) Lee Robinson's wife, Julia Buckingham, still lives on Buckingham property north of the village. Their two sons are: Harry, who lives with his wife, Evelyn, and son in Terrace Park; and John, who lives with his mother, together with his wife Verona and David and Jack, sons of a former marriage.

(4) Elias Robinson married Ida Denman. (5) Jim Robin-

son's wife was named Alice. (6) and (7) The sisters Lizzie and Flora married Dick Thayer and Joe McKinsey respectively.[69]

Mrs. Alice RUFF and her husband lived at the corner of Jackson and Kilgore. There were two Ruff children: J. Aylett (who died when a young man) and Ella. Ella first married Ed Greenfield, and later a man named Edwards. She died of cancer. They were active in the church and Ella left the Methodist organization $1000 upon her death in 1922.

The SHIVELY family lived on the Buckingham farm in early 1900's when the children were small. They then removed to Miamiville but two of the grandchildren are now living here again. There were seven children: (1) Kate Kelch who has five children; (2) Hazel Motsinger who has two; (3) Myrtle who was married to Ed McAfee, had two children and who died young; (4) Everett (deceased), who had three children; (5) L. Ellsworth who was killed by an automobile in 1943; (6) Ezra; and (7) Ben who married Margarette McGuire and lived for some years in the big Queal house near the Miamiville bridge. They had one son Stanley who did not live long, and two daughters. Margaret is married to Charles SCHMIDT and lives in House No. 162 (Illus. 49). They have four children — Cheryl, Bonnie, Charles and Steven. Juanita, the other daughter, is married to Eugene TINGLEY and they also live on Camp Road. They have two sons, Kim and Michael. Both of these girls and their families are a big asset to the community and the church.[70]

Sarah SOUTHWORTH, the daughter of Mrs. Theresa Brown, married Earl WARTNABY in New York in 1908 and they came back here to live. They bought the house on the hill (No. 153) from the W. P. O'Hara estate, the same year their daughter, Violet Virginia, was born. Mr. and Mrs. Wartnaby were later divorced. Violet attended the University of Cincinnati and had two daughters by her first husband, Bernard Skor: Sally who died while still a baby and Jeanne who graduated from Indian Hill High School in 1955. Violet and Bernard were divorced and he died not long after. She later married Robert Greene, former school teacher.[71]

Leonidas L. and Harriet Delany TITTLE came here in 1875 with three children: Ella, Alice and Nellie. Ella married Thomas BURCHILL, a descendant of one of the pioneering families. His home was on a farm south of the village where the Gants now live. Ella and Thomas had eight children. Willie and Elsie died as children and Harry died when twenty-one. The married names of the other girls were: Alice Sellers, Nancy Britt, Ella Tate, Harriet Kroger, and Jenny Teitke. Nancy Burchill Britt had two daughters, Vernice and Pearl. Vernice is married to William Fischer and has five children.

Alice Tittle married George McGinnis and had one child who died while quite young. Nellie Tittle married Arthur Lewis (see Lewis family).

Mr. and Mrs. Tittle and their daughters were mainstays of the Methodist Church and this interest continues today with their descendants who still live here. Mrs. Nellie Lewis and Hazel Robinson work with the Women's Society, and Allan Wogenstahl is currently church organist.[72]

Dr. Jacob THEIL was a resident of Camp Dennison a short time. He lived at the corner of Cunningham and Route 126, a house now owned by Mr. and Mrs. Joe Faul.[73]

George and Anna WAITS moved here in 1907 and lived in House No. 140 on Camp Road until they died in 1923 and 1924. They are buried in Miamiville. They had six children, two of whom are living in Camp Dennison at the present time, Ella Mae who is the widow of Clair T. Yeager, and Audrey who is married to William F. (Fred) Eggers and who has one son, William Jr. Helen played the organ and piano in the church for many years, she is married to Frank DeAngelo and lives in Hyde Park, Cincinnati Ohio; she has two children, Barbara Ann Crump and Frank Jr. Harry is married to Irene Breyer and lives in Buffalo, New York. Laura is the widow of George Burroughs and lives in Norwood, Ohio; and Frank, who is married to Eva Wharton and has one daughter, Margaret Ann, lives near Mt. Orab, Ohio.[74]

Mr. and Mrs. Bert WALLS came here in 1912 to go into business with William Eberhardt. However, this proved unsatisfactory and they purchased from Mrs. Bayless the house on Lincoln where Mrs. Walls still lives. They bred, boarded and showed cocker spaniels and became highly respected by dog fanciers of greater Cincinnati. Mrs. Shattuck, Mrs. Walls' mother, lived with them before her death. Bert Walls died a few years ago.[75]

Richard and Nettie WEBER owned the house which Dorothea Dority now owns along the railroad track (No. 10). Their daughter, Nellie Weber Conklin, lives in California. Their son, Dick, died when a small boy. They also raised a niece, Edna Thompson, who married Cecil Reese.[76]

Mr. Edward WILEY with his family moved here in 1902. There were four children in the family. Minor now married to Mildred Siefert, lives in Milford and has one son, Ronald. Helen, the wife of Fred Grau, had four children, Helen Elizabeth, Otto W. who was killed in World War II, Fred Jr. and Mildred Virginia. Harold graduated from Denison University and completed his medical studies abroad, is now an obstetrician and lives in Terrace Park, Ohio; he is married to Mary Moore and has one daughter. Mildred is the wife of Ray Cannon and lives in Los Angeles, California. They have two sons, Douglas and George. The Wiley family regularly attended church and Sunday School and were very active in the musical activities of the church.[77]

Mr. and Mrs. William WHITELOCK lived in House No. 155 (Illus. 49). Mr. Whitelock was the successful bidder when the Methodist church was moved from below the hill to its present location. His brother Ed lived in the Price house which stood between House No. 148 and No. 149 (Illus. 49). Mrs. William Whitelock had two daughters, Katy and Millie Barnett. Katy married a Mr. Ginn and had a daughter Katie, who was raised by her grandmother. Millie married Hamilton C. THOMPSON and they lived in House No. 139 on Camp Road; they had one son Orville. Mr. and Mrs. Thompson were active in church work and at one time Mr. Thompson was Sunday School Superintendent. After his first wife died he married Polly Doll but they had no children. H. C. Thompson's father lived in House No. 99 on the main highway where Morris Walton now lives.[78]

Mr. E. E. WILLIAMS was a school teacher here in 1898. He had a son Rae and a daughter Ada. His sister-in-law, Anna M. RIGGS, lived with them while teaching school in Washington Heights (now Indian Hill). The whole family attended Sunday School regularly. Miss Riggs was also active in church and was organist for some time.

Ike WILLIAMS and his wife lived on Daniels St. (House No. 148). Their four sons were William, Stanley, George and Everett. Across the street from the Williams' lived Daisy Hannah, her mother and two sisters. When Mrs. Hannah died, Daisy went to live with the Williams family. After Mr. and Mrs. Williams were divorced, Ike and Daisy were married and had one son, Joseph, who is an attorney in Cincinnati.[79]

1. Letter from a great-granddaughter of Daniel Price, Mrs. Jessie Price Lytle of St. Petersburg, Florida.
2. Plats, Hamilton County Courthouse, Cincinnati, Ohio. Book 620, page 122.
3. Account books in the possession of Mrs. Edith Knicely. Mrs. Knicely also has Symmes Township reports for 1870-1884 and public school fund records from 1870-71.
4. A book of Township maps owned by Lola Bonnell.
5. Information from Mrs. Mayme Leiman and Mr. Howard Brown.
6. Information obtained from Henry Cordes through Mabel Kinney and Edwin S. Kinney.
7. Records of the Mt. Olivet Baptist Church.
8. Source of information — Morris Walton.
9. Source — Mrs. Gladys Mundy, Cincinnati.
10. Source — Mr. Bill Cisco.
11. Source — Mrs. Esther Broadus.
12. Source — Mrs. Hester Ferguson.
13. Source — Mrs. Eliza Davis.

14. Source — Richard Frazier.
15. Source — Dr. Rolf Pinkvoss
16. Source — Church records.
17. Source — Mrs. Elva Maphet.
18. Source — Mrs. Elva Maphet.
19. Source — Mrs. Donna Eveland, Terrace Park.
20. Source — Mrs. Velma Specker, Terrace Park.
21. Source — Mrs Josephine Benken Bauer.
22. Source — Mrs. Sarah Wartnaby.
23. Source — Mr. Byran Brunner.
24. Source — Mrs. Rose Holmes, Loveland, Ohio.
25. Source — Mrs. Edna Howard, Columbus, Ohio.
26. Source — Mr. William Baumheckel, Indianapolis, Indiana.
27. Source — Mrs. Harry Carter.
28. Source — Mrs. Gertrude Little.
29. Source — Mrs. Mary Smith.
30. Source — Mr. Oren Compton, Jr., Norwood, Ohio.
31. Source — Mrs. Clara Winkelman.
32. Source — Mrs. Nellie Lewis
33. Source — Mrs. Ruth Brunner, Philadelphia, Penna.
34. Source — Miss Effie Daughters, Milford, Ohio.
35. Source — Mrs. Nellie Lewis.
36. *The Elliot Families* 1762-1911, compiled by Simon Elliot, Princeton, Illinois, 1911.
37. Source — Mrs. Joseph Faul.
38. Source — Mrs. Mamie Fischer.
39. Source — Mrs. Gladys James.
40. Source — Mr. Allan Fry.
41. Source — Louis Adams.
42. Source — Miss Alma Green.
43. Source — Mrs. Florence Pinkvoss.
44. Source — Mr. and Mrs. Porter Hancock.
45. Source — Mrs. William Hartzell.
46. Source — Mrs. Julia Robinson.
47. Source — Mrs. Pearl Yungblutt.
48. Source — Mrs. Florence Pinkvoss.
49. Source — Mrs. Edith Knicely.
50. Source — Mrs Catherine Wood, Williams Corner, Ohio.
51. Source — Mr. Richard Leever.
52. Source — Mrs. Mayme Leiman.
53. Source — Mrs. Nellie Lewis.
54. Source — Mrs. Norman Little and Mrs. Hallie Armacost.
55. Source — Mr. Willard Bayless, Wenatchee, Washington.
56. Source — Mrs. Eva Cosby, Florida.
57. Source — Mrs. Sarah Wartnaby.
58. Source — Mrs. Ruth Whitaker, Mason, Ohio.
59. Source — Mrs. Grace Pierce, Sharonville, Ohio.
60. Source — Mrs. Lillie Schwartz.
61. Source — Mrs. Frances Eigher.

62. Source — Mrs. Ruth Jeffries, Covington, Ky.
63. Source — Mrs. Florence Pinkvoss.
64. Source — Mrs. Florence Pinkvoss.
65. Source — Mrs. Florence Pinkvoss.
66. Source — Mrs. Florence Pinkvoss.
67. Source — Mrs. Florence Pinkvoss.
68. Source — Mrs. Florence Pinkvoss.
69. Source — Mrs. Julia Robinson.
70. Source — Mrs. Margaret Schmidt.
71. Source — Mrs. Sarah Wartnaby.
72. Source — Mrs. Nellie Lewis.
73. Source — Dr. Rolf Pinkvoss.
74. Source — Ella Mae Yeager.
75. Source — Mrs. Sarah Wartnaby.
76. Source — Mrs. Nellie Lewis.
77. Source — Mrs. Mildred Cannon.
78. Source — Church records and Mrs. Julia Robinson.
79. Source — Mrs. Sarah Wartnaby.

Chapter V

THE METHODIST CHURCH

*"The World, the Devil and Tom Paine!
Have done their best but all in vain,
They can't prevail, the reason is
The Lord defends the Methodist."*
—Early American saying.

The first meeting of the Methodist Society in our village was held in the cabin of Henry Stroman in 1806. According to a talk made by Smith B. Quayle at a rededication of the church on April 25, 1926, Peter Cartwright, a well known circuit rider, called "The Preacher on Horseback," preached at that meeting.

It is believed that this Methodist Society was an outgrowth of the Milford church, which was first organized in 1797. For purposes of organization, the General Conference had listed the Methodists of Clermont and parts of two adjoining counties as belonging at Milford and in 1805-6 was considered to have a membership of 750. It is probable that the members of the Society at Big Bottom (which was the name used by Christian Waldsmith) were counted in this membership.

In fact, the Trustees' Minute Book for the Milford Church on the date of February 16, 1818, lists Henry Stroman as being chosen to be a Trustee of the Milford Church.

After 1806 Methodist church services were held in homes, the Kugler School House on Kugler Mill Road (now Galbraith Road) and various places. There is a church building shown on the map of the village in the year 1844. However, this church was a log building erected by Mr. Waldsmith soon after his arrival here and where he preached on Sundays. His father was a minister in the German Reformed church in Pennsylvania and it is reasonable to assume that this was a German Reformed church. Mr. Waldsmith was very active in this church, not only preaching but teaching religion during the week. Prior to the Civil War, there are records indicating that this church was still standing but no services had been held there for some fifteen years and the members had joined what was called the "Milford Methodists."

During the early years of the Methodist Church in this area, the work of the church was carried on by itinerant ministers called Circuit Riders. Because of the extent of territory covered, the circuit rider came infrequently — many weeks elapsing between his visits. During that interval, services were conducted by a "local preacher." He worked six days a week, as other men did, and then preached on Sunday.

During the period from 1800 to 1816 the Circuit Rider received $80.00 per year and traveling expenses. If they were married, the wife received an annual allowance of $80.00. Each child up to the age of 7 received $16.00 per year and for a child from 7 to 14 years of age, $24.00 per year.[1]

Although he may have been lax in attending "local preaching," the old time Methodist never missed his Quarterly meeting when the itinerant preacher and the presiding Elder came — and sometimes even the Bishop. These meetings lasted two days, and it was a great time for "visiting."

Preaching began on Saturday at 10 or 11 o'clock in the morning. A short service was held in the afternoon, after which

Methodist Church — 1918.

the Quarterly Conference was convened. On Sunday morning the Love Feast was held, conducted by one of the preachers, and about 11 o'clock the principal sermon of the Quarterly meeting was preached by the Presiding Elder, followed by a sermon, and then perhaps by an exhortation. The sacraments of baptism and the Lord's Supper were usually administered at the close of the morning services, though sometimes deferred till the afternoon. At night there was again preaching — generally followed by prayer meeting, exhortation to repentance, collects for penitent seekers, and stirring hymns.[2]

The later camp meetings were an evolution from these gatherings. Epworth Heights, near Branch Hill, is the one best remembered in this area.

There must have been such a meeting at our church in 1857 as in the Bible on the altar in the church at the present time there is a pencil notation signed by Wm. Herr, who was Presiding Elder of the East Cincinnati District from 1855 to 1858, as follows:

"W. Herr was born in Hagerstown, Md., March 9, 1806. *Born again* by the spirit of God, Sep. 25, 1827. This morning, May 30, 1857, in Love Feast for Madisonville Charge, my soul rejoices in God my Saviour, and through the blood of Christ hope for everlasting life. Glory to God we have a good meeting. May the Lord pour His spirit on the church."

Going back to our local church, there was a permanent class meeting organized in the early church with Henry Stroman as class leader. Isaac Ebbert was the traveling preacher and according to the Conference Minutes he was assigned to the Georgetown Circuit.

In the list of preachers and circuit riders appearing in the Appendix, preachers are listed for both the Milford and Madison, or Miami Circuits, inasmuch as it is believed that, although separate services were held in our village, the local Society, until the church was built in 1845, was not considered as a separate entity by the Conference and was thought of as part of the Milford church. Hence the expression of earlier records as "Milford Methodists."

The next authentic record is of a meeting called in Kugler's School House May 10, 1845. Continuing Mr. Quayle's speech, we read:

"At a meeting of the committee Henry Stroman, Eleazer Campbell, James Simmons, appointed by the third Quarterly Conference of Madison Circuit, Ohio Conference, to estimate the cost of a new church proposed to be built at Kuglers. All members present. The committee decided a suitable church could be built for nine hundred dollars."

Then follows, "At a meeting held at the residence of M. Kugler on Friday, the 15th of May, 1845, the following persons present: M. Kugler, E. Campbell, Jeremiah Price, Smith Buckingham, H. Stroman, T. Keith and H. Packard. The following persons were duly appointed Trustees for the Methodist Church at Kuglers. John Kugler, Jeremiah Price, Eleazer Campbell, Henry Stroman and Smith Buckingham. The Trustees assembled resolved to forthwith circulate a paper for the purpose of securing funds to build a church on a lot already deeded to the Board of Trustees by M. Kugler for that puropse. They further resolved to meet at Kugler's School House on Saturday next to let out the building provided a sufficient amount had been obtained by that date."

The next report shows men had speed in those days. "At an adjourned meeting of the Trustees held at Kugler's School House on Saturday, May 24th, 1845, the following present. E. Campbell, Henry Stroman, Smith Buckingham, and E. Ebbitt, the latter in the chair. The members reported eight hundred dollars subscribed. This being a sufficient amount they let the house. M. Kugler was present and proposed to build the house for one thousand dollars, which offer the Trustees accepted. They also appointed E. Campbell and Henry Stroman a committee together with Mr. Williamson (M. Kugler's builder) to arrange a plan. They to pay him five hundred dollars on or before the 20th of August and the balance on or before the 21st of November 1845."

Mr. Quayle was quoting from the old church records which were last in his possession and unfortunately have been lost or destroyed.

His speech continued:

"The complete subscription list is recorded in the old book. It is a roll of honor of that day, containing 153 names. Mathias Kugler who gave the lot and contracted to build the church, heads the list for $200.00. Down near the end of that honorable

Rev. Raymond Deweese at pulpit during church services.
Photo by Rob Paris.

list I find the name of John Kugler, son of Mathias, who gave $200.00. The Kugler family gave the lot, built the church, and gave nearly one half of the estimated cost in cash."

The church was located on the east side of Milford-Glendale Road (Rt. 126) below the cemetery hill, where the public township pump was located. The well is still there but there is no pump.

Mr. Quayle continued: "The Methodist Society worshipped in this church until the old order had completely changed. A great war had been fought and won by the North. Kugler's was forgotten in the new fame and glory of Camp Dennison. Many buildings and residences at Kugler's were bought by the Government and moved to Camp Dennison."

During the period that the training camp was here, it is possible that no church services were held for the residents of the village. Nathaniel C. Callendar, a member of the Milford Quarterly Conference, was appointed by the Cincinnati Conference to serve as Chaplain of the Army at Camp Dennison in 1863, 1864 and 1865.

This conclusion is reached because of the following:

During the fifties, in the Annual Conference Minutes of the Cincinnati Conference for the Madisonville Circuit, a detailed collection for missions is listed and the following names appear under the name of Germany: Mrs. Nancy Buckingham, J. Price, S. Buckingham, H. Stroman, H. Leever, Susan Price, Lydia Umphlet, and Elizabeth Price.

In 1856, 1857 and 1858 the following names were added, under the name of Germany: J. Turney, S. S. Umphlet, Maria Buckingham, Miss A. Stroman, J. Gest, J. C. Fogleman, J. Stroman, J. S. Price. Jane Buckingham, Mrs. Turney, Mrs. E. R. Shults, Miss S. E. Shults, G. W. Shults, Miss R. J. Shults, Miss E. C. Shults, Phebe Stroman, T. Wiley, Nancy Fitzwaller (Fitzwater), E. S. Pollock, G. S. Pollock, Silas Riggs, R. S. M'Calmont, H. G. Wasson, Eliza Ware, Margaret Gest, Samantha Ware, Jane Queal, Elizabeth Turney, John Queal, W. S. Lever, G. S. Rinner, Paul Riggs, James Denison, N. Buckingham, D. Cotton and H. Staman (may be Stroman).

However, in 1862, Germany is not listed, but Miamiville is and familiar names appear as donating to missions: J. D. Leonard, J. Price, Mrs. Harrison, J. Gest, S. Buckingham, Mrs. Price, John Woodlief, S. Woodlief, W. D. Courts, P. Day, J. H. Thompson, N. Sanders, Nancy Fitzwater, and Maggie Fitzwater.

In the conference of 1866, however, a new charge called the Camp Dennison and Indian Hill was formed and N. C. Callendar was appointed as preacher. At the conference of 1867 this charge made the following report: 47 members; 1 death; 42 probationers; no baptisms; two churches; probable value of property $2500.00.

In 1868 under the Madisonville charge we are listed as Camp Dennison and the following people donated to missions: Rosa Stroman, Sarah Price, Mrs. Riggs, W. Warbleton, Mrs. Forward, A. Stroman, Mrs. Buckingham, Miss M. Quail, Mrs. Simpson, G. Stroman, F. Burdsall, S. Buckingham, J. Price, J. Quail, J. S. Vosburg, William Beard and S. Simpson. In 1871, the following additional names appear: Mrs. Kiser, John Sullivan, W. Brown, Mr. Kiser, James Armstrong, George Simpson, Dan Reddy, George Quail, Joe Sugart and C. Buckingham.

Going back to Mr. Quayle: "Turning the pages of the old record I come to this 'Camp Dennison, September 8, 1867. Pursuant to instructions from the Pastor, Rev. W. Q. Shannon, we the members and Trustees do hereby meet for the purpose of considering the removal of the building now owned and occupied as a Methodist Church, and to purchase suitable lots in Camp Dennison to place the building thereon. Present, J. Price, Smith Buckingham, F. Peckenpaugh, G. Simpson and S. Vosburg. The above named Trustees were appointed to superintend the moving and to have charge of all details including raising money by subscription. Signed W. Q. Shannon, Preacher and G. A. Simpson, Clerk.'"

Lots 39 and 40 (each 50 feet wide) of Herman and Brauneis Subivision located on Jackson Street, 150 feet west of Charles Alley and extending one hundred forty feet to Jefferson Alley

Interior of Methodist Church during Sunday School. Dick Leever, Superintendent. The cross in the front of the room was made and donated by Earl Howell, Sr.   Photo by Rob Paris.

in the rear, were purchased from George D. Hermann and Enrich J. Brauneis on June 3, 1868 by the Trustees, namely Smith Buckingham, Jeremiah Price, Hiram Leever, Frederick Peckenpaugh, William Beard, George A. Simpson and S. S. Vosburg. This deed is in the church records.

The specifications were recorded June 9th, 1868.

"To all whom it may concern. Sealed proposals for bids will now be received and closed Saturday, June 13th, 1868, for the removal of the Methodist Church now located on a lot belonging to the Church. To be taken down, moved and rebuilt on lots 39 and 40 in Herman and Brauneis Subdivision in

Camp Dennison. To be completed at the earliest possible moment. The following will be strictly adhered to; and the bid to be given to the lowest responsible bidder. We reserve the right to reject any and all bids.

"Original building, 28 feet wide by 38 feet long to be rebuilded with an addition of ten feet to be added to the length of the building. Entire new roof on building which shall project 18 inches with boxed moulding finish. Entire building to be newly weatherboarded. Building to be painted with three coats of paint mixed with oil and white lead. Shutters to be painted green. The interior to be plastered with a three coat finish. The doors now in old building to be made new. The inside of the Church to be altered with new style pulpit, with pillars for lights at each side of the platform. Eight new seats to be made fourteen feet long to be placed four on each side of the platform. New floor for the entire length and width of the room. A brick flue for stove pipe. Two new windows with shutters making in all eight windows in entire building. A cupola for the bell eight feet high and five feet square with post columns. Also two or three new steps."

Mr. Quayle's speech continues:

"On June 13, 1868 the bid of Wm. Whitelock for $850.00 was duly accepted and he furnished three bondsmen to guarantee the job. The amount was raised by subscription and all the names are duly recorded."

"There were no major improvements until August, 1899, when the church building was generally renovated at a cost of $109.00. The present pulpit and chairs were bought at that time. The pulpit was new but the chairs came from the Lockland Methodist Church.

"In 1919, because the building was in bad repair, Horatio Buckingham circulated a subscription paper and went only to the families who did not belong to the church. He collected $191.50 and the church was repaired, reroofed and placed in good condition. That was the year when the church began to be called a Community Church."

In 1922 there became available a bequest of one thousand dollars from Ella Ruff, who had been a member of the church all her life. A part of the fund was used that year to build the present vestibule on the building. The church was also wired for electricity around 1923 and the old gas lights which had to be pumped were abandoned. The church paid only for the materials used in the wiring of the church, the labor being donated by Albert Flint, the husband of Roma Buckingham, and Clifford (Sam) Jackson.

In 1925 another bequest came to the church. Joseph Haffenbradl. who was not a member but who lived on the farm on

Kugler Mill Road at the end of Camp Road, remembered the church in his will to the amount of $2500.00 in Cincinnati Gas & Electric shares. This fund was left in trust with the Cincinnati Methodist Union in perpetuity, the interest to be paid to the Trustees of Camp Dennison Church for one and only one purpose, namely the minister's salary. At the present time the church is receiving $100.00 a year from this fund.

Around 1925, Mr. and Mrs. Hereward Fry gave the community house to the church. This was originally the yeast house of Herman Fischer and then was the Fry's chicken house.

Community House on Methodist Church grounds.   Photo by Rob Paris.

In 1926 there was a general renovation of the church and it was at the rededication of the church on completion of this work that Mr. Quayle made this speech regarding the history. His speech closed with the following:

"Now we come to the latest evidence of the love of this community for their old church. There was a considerable balance in the Ella Ruff fund which was available for the physical upkeep of the church. The Trustees and the Ladies Aid Society met in joint session to consider the needs of the church. The ceiling which had been on for 57 years was in bad order. It was decided to remove it and place a metal ceiling on the room. The walls were also in bad order. The old wainscoting had become unsightly. It is significant of these advanced times that women are mentioned for the first time in this record. Always before the men did the job. I have my suspicions that the women had a lot to say to the men in the old days even if their names did not get into the big book. The women who met with the Trustees to consider this last improvement were Mrs. Julia Robinson, Mrs. Herman Haller, Mrs Jennie B. Queal and Mrs. Emma C. Quayle. Mrs. Robinson was President of the Aid Society. The members of that splendid Society assumed approximately $80.00 of the expense out of their treasury. The Trustees paid for the materials and the new ceiling. The ceiling was put on by George Linke (of Milford) on his bid of $75.00. Nearly all the other labor was donated by men of the community. These men were Arnold (Tom) Barrere, Albert Lauderman, Eddie Benken, Norman Little, Lee Robinson, John Robinson, Charles Anderson, Percy Moore, Wilbur Myers, Will Ritchie, Jim Ritchie, Billie Fischer, Porter Hancock, Herman Haller, Joe Faul, Horatio Buckingham and Lloyd Lewis. Ed Leiman donated materials. The old clock that had had a long rest was repaired and cleaned by Fred B. Schaforth, the optician of Milford, and donated to the church. The total cost of these changes in the church will not be much over $200.00. If the labor were paid for at present schedules the cost would be over $500.00. Only one or two of this fine list of men belong to the church, but they show their loyalty to the community and the church by giving their time and skill without stint until the job was done. This, after all, is the real test of good citizenship."

The American flag in the church was made by hand by Mrs. Sarah Vandever Buckingham in 1929 in her 82nd year.

In 1930, the three lots adjoining the church on the east, which the church had been using through the courtesy of Mr. Smith B. Quayle and Mr. William Queal, sole heirs of John Queal, were offered to the church for $150.00. After consideration of the Board of Trustees, it was decided to purchase these lots. Fifty dollars of this amount was paid by the Sunday School, fifty dollars by the Ladies Aid Society, and the balance was subscribed by Minor Wiley, Wilbur Myers, Minnie Hancock, Leona E. Hancock, Edith Knicely, H. H. Fry, Gladys Hutchinson, Henry Pitser, Bill Knicely, Clem McGohan, Marcia L. Buckingham, R. D. Pinkvoss, Norman Little, Henry M. Pinkvoss, Mr. Fletcher, Lee Robinson, Bill Falgner, Mary Cochran, Mrs. Cochran, Velma Faul, Edw. Leiman, Hazel Lewis, Mrs. R. Bayer, Chas. S. Pierce, Porter Hancock, David Paxton.

Minor Wiley was appointed athletic director in full charge of the lots with authority to organize the young people, for utilization of the grounds as an athletic field. Several years prior to this purchase, the young people of the church and the community had combined their talents and labor and constructed a tennis court on these lots, and this offered pleasure and recreation to all the young people. Since that time various games have been played on these grounds and at the present time there is a baseball field.

In 1937 arrangements were made with the Hamilton County Board of Elections for the use of the Community House as a polling place for all elections. It is still being used for that purpose.

In September 1937 a bequest of $200.00 was left the church by Miss Emma Van Pelt, an aunt of Miss Marcia Buckingham, who made her home with Miss Buckingham in Camp Dennison for many years. In December 1937, Miss Marcia Buckingham donated to the church the framed historic picture of old Camp Dennison, this picture to hang on the church wall forever as a reminder of the great Civil War military camp.

Rev. Deweese greeting members of congregation after services.
Photo by Rob Paris.

In December 1938 an agreement was made with the Indian Hill School District to use the Community House for the primary grades while the Camp Dennison school was being repaired. Certain improvements were made in the Community House and were paid for by the School District. A new floor was laid in the front room and the walls and ceiling were covered with Celotex. The doors between the front room and back room were changed from sliding doors to hinged doors with locks.

In 1947, Miss Marcia Buckingham, a descendant of one of the original settlers and a daughter of Dr. Alfred Buckingham, died, leaving the church four lots west of and adjoining the church property and three lots immediately across Jackson Street. The money from these lots to be used for the maintenance of the church property. These lots were sold in 1953 to Ohio Homes, Inc. and the money put in the building treasury. Seven houses have been erected on these lots.

During the winter of 1954 and 1955 a new electric OrgaSonic Baldwin organ was purchased for the church, for a price of $1400.00. The young people of the church started talking of this project and solicitation was made of the community. Through a generous contribution from Mrs. Emma Fletcher Doermann, a former resident of the village, and a daughter of Mr. and Mrs. H. B. Fletcher, in whose memory this gift was given, cash was paid for this instrument. The organ was dedicated on February 13, 1955.

During the years, necessary maintenance of the church and community house has been carried on through the efforts of the Ladies Aid Society or as it is called now the Woman's Society of Christian Service, the Trustees, the Sunday School, and the various young people's societies.

On October 9, 1955 (the first day of Fire Prevention Week) the chimney of the church caught fire during services. Through the efficient work of the Miamiville Volunteer Fire Department the fire was confined to the west wall of the church around and below the chimney. A contract had just been let for the redecoration of the church and the men of the congregation had bought materials to extend the altar to both sides of the church and to lay a new floor, so this work was postponed until the wall of the church was repaired and a new chimney erected. Church and Sunday School services were held in the Community House while this work was in progress but the work is now all complete and it is a beautiful job. Besides the Trustees, those helping in the work were Earl Howell, Jr., Dick Leever, Frank and Eugene Tingley, Fred Eggers and Allan Wogenstahl. The redecorating was done by Harry B. Robinson of Terrace Park.

The outside of the church and community house had been painted in 1954 by Henry Pitser.

The present Trustees of the church are **William Gant, Earl Howell, Wilbur Myers, Norman Little, Russell Robe, and Eugene Tingley.**

The current minister is Raymond Deweese, who lives with his wife and two of his children in nearby Miamiville.

ORGANIZATIONS OF THE CHURCH

Bible Classes

A Bible Class is first mentioned as being organized in the early church with Henry Stroman as class leader. No further record is available until February 8, 1869, when the Camp Dennison Bible Class was organized. The constitution and by-laws of this organization are interesting. They voted to pay the sexton, S. P. Forward, 25c for each night that the class met to light up and warm up the church. The lights used coal oil.

Since that time there have been many men's and women's Bible classes. In the records there is a secretary's book of the Mizpah class which was organized by the women on February 13, 1935.

Musical Organizations

Music has always been important in the Methodist Church since the days of Charles Wesley who wrote many of our well known hymns, such as "Hark! The Herald Angels Sing," "A Charge To Keep I Have," and "Christ the Lord is Risen Today."

In the early days when officers of the Sunday School were elected, a chorister to lead the congregation in singing was also elected. On January 22, the following note was written to the Sunday School Board:

> "As my voice poor in singing, it is impossible for me to serve the school as chorister. I therefore resign the same.
>
> Lou M. Connett"

In January 1889 a Singing Club was organized in the church with Charles Peckenpaugh as President, Julia Buckingham, Treasurer, and Lela Marsh, Secretary. Some of the members besides the above were Lillie Buckingham, Mary Stokes, Harold Fry, Jennie Orr, Miss Vaughan, Alonzo Thompson, Mrs. Beard, Nellie Fletcher, Minnie Drake, Mr. Vaughan.

There have been volunteer choirs in the church most of the time during the years. Mrs. Herman Haller played the organ and piano and directed the choir for a good many years, and was active until her health would not permit her to play or take an active part.

There have been many faithful pianists during the years, who came and played whether it inconvenienced them or not. Some of these follow: Harold Longley (1869-70-74); Lillie Ellis (1871-72-73); Mary Bell Arthur (relative of the minister); Julia Hoffman (1873); Jennie Orr (1879-81); Ella Ruff (1884); Erma Marsh (1895-1900); T. J. Euens; Anna Riggs (1900-01);

Lillie Drake (1901); Miss Katie Ginn (1893); Lou Connett (1894); Mrs. Allen (1901-1905); Bessie Thompson (1906-1909); Frances Peteler (1911-12); Mrs. Edna Pinkvoss (1910); Helen Waits (1916-1927); Edna Thompson (1903); Dorothy Baird (1928); Helen Ausman (1928-1930); Vivian Wiggins (1930-31); Violet Wartnaby (1932); Leona Hancock (1932-1940); Mildred Frankenberg (1941); Mrs. Herman Haller (1941-52); Doris Oligee (1941-1946); Carolyn Dority (1949); Allen Wogenstahl (1953-56).

The Sunday School

The Sunday School has always been an important part of the church organization. Even during the periods when no regular preacher was assigned to the church, the Sunday School remained active.

The first official records of the Sunday School available after the church was moved to its present location in 1868 are the minutes of the regular Sunday School service on August

Allan Wogenstahl at organ of church.   Photo by Rob Paris.

21, 1870, although the Sabbath School is mentioned in the minutes of the Union Bible Class which was formed in February 1869. However, in another book is a list of the books received by S. S. Vosburg as Librarian of Camp Dennison M. E. Sunday School March 1st, 1868.

G. A. Simpson was elected Superintendent of the Sunday School at that meeting in August, 1870, Jas. Holmes, Asst. Superintendent, W. H. Queal, Secretary, W. G. Vaughn, Asst. Secretary, Maria Queal, Treasurer, S. S. Vosburg, Librarian, and Mrs. Sallie Buckingham, Asst. Librarian. The attendance is not given for that particular Sunday. However, the following

Sunday there was an attendance of three teachers and fifty-four scholars. Contribution nothing. At this meeting, Superintendent Simpson tried to resign but his resignation was not accepted. The Assistant Superintendent did resign and S. S. Vosburg was elected in his place and F. Cunningham was elected Librarian. It might be of interest to know the names of the Sunday School members at that time. They were:

Infant Class: Helen Cunningham, Alma Cunningham, Willie Sullivan, Tom Sullivan, Henry Brown, Tom Brown, Solomon Burchill, Walter Ferris, George Fox, George Snyder, Charles Price, Maggie Kizer, Jessie Kizer, Emma Vosburg, Cora Ludlow, Kate Campbell, Lillie Longley, Carrie Young, Hattie Bush, Misses Thompson and John King, Maggie King, Katie King, Osher Price.

Testament Class No. 2: John Queal, Harold Longley, Charles Kizer, Charles Vandiver, Ed Leever, Horatio Paxton, Albert Paxton, Tom Burchill, Charles Vosburg, Millard Vosburg, Walter Price.

Testament Class No. 1: Charles Peckenpaugh, Ada Fitzwater, Minty Queal, Milly Barnett, Ida Price, Lizzie Brown, Mary Brown, Carrie Snyder, Lillie Fox, Mamie Bush.

Bible Class No. 2, Female: W. H. Queal, Jennie Burchill, Jennie Brown, Mrs. Burchill, Annie Snyder, Rosa Stroma (Stroman), Katie Wright, Annie Stroma (Stroman), Kate Barnett, Mrs. V. Buckingham.

Bible Class No. 1, Male: W. Beard, F. Peckenpaugh, M. S. Price, S. Losh, C. Peckenpaugh, John Burchill.

The Sunday School at that time met at 2 o'clock in the afternoon and the attendance was very good — usually ranging from 40 to 60. On February 19, 1871 there were 88 people present. The collections were very poor however and it is hard to understand how they met their expenses. The collections were most generally less than a dollar and usually less than fifty cents. On August 21, 1870 there was a balance in the treasury of $8.10, but during the years lesson leaves, Bibles, new hymn books, and new books for the library were bought.

The purchase of the first organ was instigated through the Sunday School when on April 23, 1871 a committee of three was appointed to inquire as to the price of an organ. This was amended for committee to be instructed to procure an organ and have it placed in the church. Committee: Mrs. Edsel, Simpson, Denham and Mrs. Hamilton. Church records reveal that in July 1872 a Style 59 F & F organ was purchased from D. H. Baldwin, dealer in Pianos, Organs and Melodeons, 158 West Fourth St., Cincinnati, for the purchase price of $125.00. This amount was secured by small donations from the members during the preceding year. Receipted bill is in the records of the church.

In the Sunday School book under date of February 19, 1882, there is a notation that a new organ was received on February 18, 1882. There is no other mention of this organ except that a concert for organ was given in January 1882.

In 1871 the Sunday School is listed for a couple of weeks as Grand Valley Sunday School.

During the early 1880's the minutes of each Sunday School session contained a weather report.

Attendance dropped in 1884 and 1885 to between 15 and 30 with an average of 20. By 1887 the attendance was better,

Methodist Church, 1955, with Community House in background.
Photo by Rob Paris.

ranging from 30 to 50. Collections had picked up a little — some times they took in over a dollar. The attendance was still being counted by male and female, so many male teachers and so many male scholars, so many female teachers and so many female scholars.

The official business of the Sunday School during these years was conducted by the Sunday School Board composed of the officers and teachers of the Sunday School. This board sometimes met on Sunday and sometimes on another day of the week. In January 1888 there must have been a particularly spirited meeting. Mr. Talbott was elected by the Sunday School to be Superintendent. However, the election had to be sanctioned by the Board and at its meeting, Mr. Albert Connett and Mrs. Howren (the minister's wife) were nominated but the latter declined the nomination. On the second ballot Mr.

Connett received only two votes, Mrs. Marshall and Mrs. Howren, the other members of the Board refusing to vote. The Pastor declared Mr. Connett superintendent.

The first mention of a Sunday School Convention was in June, 1898. Then on the first Sunday in October, 1898, the Symmes Township Sunday School Association was organized. This was composed of the Methodist churches at Camp Dennison and Washington Heights, which is the present town hall of Indian Hill Village on the northeast corner of Given and Camargo Roads, and the Remington Christian Church. All day meetings were held on the first Sunday in June and October. Smith Quayle was President of this organization for many years, and Viola Turner was Secretary.

Mention has been made previously of a book listing names of books contained in the Sunday School Library. When any officers were elected, a librarian and an assistant librarian were elected, and they were in charge of these books. Over 200 books are listed in this book which dates back to March, 1868, which was before the church was moved to its present location.

There is now a membership of 80 in the Sunday School and an average attendance of about 40, mostly children.

Many of the most faithful workers in the church have served diligently in the Sunday School, besides the recorded Sunday School Superintendents who are listed in the Appendix, many teachers served loyally for long periods of time.

Miss Bessie Thompson on the grounds of the Methodist Home in Cincinnati.

One of the most loyal members who can be remembered by many people living today is Miss Bessie Thompson. She was born in Gloversville, New York, on August 1, 1863 and her name is first mentioned in the Sunday School records in 1906. She was the organist off and on for many years, she taught a Sunday School class practically all the time, she was active in the Epworth League, and she was also janitor of the church. She lived in House No. 14 (Illus. 49). She entered the Methodist Home for the Aged in 1931 and died there in November 1946. The small study table in the church was given by her.

Women's Society of Christian Service

The women have always been active and have taken the initiative in the work of the church in Camp Dennison. Whenever money was needed by the church or there was work to be done, the women pitched right in and brought the project to a completion.

There was a Ladies' Aid Society in the church for many years but no official records can be found when the first group was organized.

In September 1940, pursuant to a change in the rules of the Methodist Church, the name of the Ladies' Aid was officially changed to the Women's Society of Christian Service. The first officers of this group were Mrs. Jennie Kindt, President; Mrs. Mary Fletcher, Vice President; Mrs. Amanda Anderson, Recording Secretary; Mrs. Genevieve Green, Treasurer; Mrs. J. P. Strong, 2nd Vice President; Mary Louise Strong, Secretary Young Peoples Work; and Emma C. Quayle, Secretary, Missionary Education.

The upkeep and maintenance of the church and community house have been a major responsibility of the women's organizations. They have seen that the buildings are kept painted, bought new equipment for the buildings as needed, and pay for the fuel used in heating the buildings.

At the present time their meetings are held on the third Wednesday of every month. The meeting is usually preceded by a covered dish lunch at noon.

Young People's Organization

There have been different young people's organizations during the years but the one of the longest duration was the Epworth League. This was first organized in the Methodist Church on May 5, 1889 in Cleveland. The official records of the Camp Dennison Church indicate that an Epworth League was organized on October 27, 1907 under the leadership of Mr. W. P. O'Hara, who was very active in all church affairs. However, an Epworth League existed in our church much previous to this inasmuch as there is a letter addressed to the Epworth League dated November 20, 1893 and signed by E. A. Greenfield, in which he tenders his resignation as a member of the Society "cause best known to myself." Another slip of paper also shows some officers and it is believed that this is for the Epworth League. President, S. B. Queal; Spiritual, Mrs. Sargent; Charity, Mrs. Anna Hill; Social, Jessie Price; Literary, Lou Connett; Secretary, Mr. Greenfield; and Treasurer, Harvey Connett.

There were 15 active members when the League was organized in 1907. These members were: Theo. E. Rammler, Treasurer, Alma A. Green, Mary A. Poe, Helen E. Wiley, Elizabeth Green, Nellie Conklin, Secretary, Delia Green, William F. Allen, Edith M. McAllister, Ollie Green, Charles M. Green, Minor Wiley, Mrs. Edna Pinkvoss, W. P. O'Hara and Bessie Thompson.

At first each member was assessed dues but in March 1908 it was decided to abolish the dues and adopt a regular collection taken once a month. The first collection recorded was in May 1908 and the amount received was 50 cents.

The first Epworth League must have been a progressive and wide awake group because in July of 1908 $60.00 was donated through a social and subscription raised by Mr. O'Hara to install a gas lighting system in the church. Money to help church projects was raised through lawnfetes and socials of different kinds.

Former members of the Epworth League will remember the Penny Drill for flowers where each member walked up front and put his money in the basket. This was first started in March 1917. It was also at this time that members were again assessed dues of 5¢ a month. Evidently the monthly collections had proved inadequate. From the records, while there was an average attendance of from 10 to 30 people, the collections that are recorded in the Secretary's book never amounted to over a dollar.

The records are very incomplete on the Epworth League but do show that its progress fluctuated during the years. There were many discussions as to what to do to attract more members and how to make the meetings more interesting. (Doesn't that sound familiar?)

The Methodist Church has now changed the name of its young people's organization to the "Methodist Youth Fellowship."

1. *History of Ohio Methodism*, by J. M. Baker. Ph.D.. Curts & Jennings, Cincinnati; Eaton & Mains. New York; 1898.
2. *Picture of Early Methodism in Ohio*. by Samuel W Willimas; Jennings & Graham, Cincinnati; Eaton & Mains, New York; 1909.

Chapter VI

THE STORY OF THE CAMP DENNISON SCHOOLS

The first indication of education in classes was the newspaper advertisement asking for "an old man able to teach a night school of reading, writing, and arithmetic" at Waldsmith's settlement in the Big Bottom.[1]

The first school house was a log building on the south side of Kugler Mill (now Galbraith Road), one half mile east of Buckingham Road. Its water was supplied by a spring which is still there. Miss Jerusha Jones taught here; we do not know how long the school existed. This information was obtained from Mrs. Jessie Price Lytle, whose father, William Price (Prisch) attended there.

The next building used as a school was the brick building on Lincoln Road at the Little Miami Railroad, southeast. (Building No. 11, Illus. No. 49). Mr. Leavin Ready was a teacher in this school. It is now used as a residence and is owned by the Knicely family.

On October 3, 1863, land was purchased from Dr. Alfred Buckingham[2] and a two story brick building was erected on Route 126, or as it was then known, Montauk Road. Presumably due to the Civil War, this building was not used until

School house prior to 1870. Now the property of Mrs. Edith Knicely.
Photo by Rob Paris.

1870. There were two class rooms on the first floor, and one large room, with a stage at one end, upstairs. The upstairs room was used as a school for the Negro children, who were taught by a Mr. Johnson. This was shortly discontinued and the pupils transferred to the first floor. The upstairs was used for school entertainments, commencements, and various community meetings.

Each of the first floor rooms had an entrance from a hall which also contained a winding stairway leading to the second floor hallway. The three rooms were at first heated by stoves, but later a furnace was placed in each downstairs room with registers above which allowed the heat to enter the second floor.

In the 1870's those wishing to attend high school after finishing the grades went to Woodward High in Cincinnati, riding the trains morning and evening. After passage of the Boxwell Law in 1896 and the Patterson Law in 1901, pupils were sent to Milford and Terrace Park High Schools, the Board of Education paying the tuition with pupils furnishing transportation. Later, the transportation was paid, or they were sent by bus.

In 1937 the district was merged with Indian Hill, including Remington, Washington Heights, Jefferson and Franklin Schools and later Concord.

In 1939 the school building was remodeled. A new furnace room provided hot water heat. Two restrooms were added, and a drinking fountain was placed in the hall, and one just outside the building. There were individual lockers for the pupils. The

Schoolhouse before remodeling.

windows were enlarged and moved to furnish more efficient lighting. While the school was being remodeled, the classes for the first four grades were held in the Camp Dennison Community House, the upper four grades went to Jefferson School on Indian Hill.

Later a building was erected on Drake Road, Indian Hill Village, and in the Fall of 1950 the pupils were transported by bus to the new school. There are now two schools in use in the district, Indian Hill and Concord; whereas there had been five before consolidation was effected.

The schools were formerly under the supervision of the Hamilton County Board of Education and Mr. C. A. Wilson, Newtown, was our District Superintendent. Indian Hill became an exempted Village School in 1951 and was placed under state supervision.

In June, 1954, the first high school commencement was held in the auditorium of the Indian Hill School. Those from Camp Dennison in this class were: Nancy Brown, Evelyn Hillard, Donald Freeman, Herbert Hillard, Richard Weaver and Allen Wogenstahl.

In 1952, the Camp Dennison School building was sold at auction to the Ohio Gravel Company, to be held for future use.

Here follows a list of teachers, to the best of our knowledge, up to 1950: Jerusha Jones, Leavin Ready, Mr. Johnson, S. T. Dial, W. P. O'Hara, Miss Perrine, Mr. Ferris, Miss Shaw, Mr. Christwell, Frank Cunningham, Frazier Acomb, John Acomb, George Nelson, Harry Nelson, William Finch, Minnie Flinchpaugh, Lela Marsh, Alonzo Thompson, Orville Sater, James McGohan, E. E. Williams, Henry Straus, Wm. J. Thompson,

Schoolhouse — 1955. Now the property of Ohio Gravel Co. Photo by Rob Paris.

Orville Manning, Earl Hutchinson, Alma Greene, Fred Leever, Stella Brown, Florence Fletcher, Ella Knicely, Porter Hancock (25 years), Minnie Hancock, Leona Hancock, Ethelyn Stivers, Bedah Henize, Dorothy Baird, Robert Greene, Harold Pricket, Ada May Kelly, Julia Schmidt, Ruth Wetterstroem, Mrs. May Eltzroth, and Leroy Eltzroth.

Music teachers: Ella Knicely, Mrs. Edith Duderstadt, Mrs. Jean Ann Reeves.

In a ledger book of Symmes Township dated 1870 and 1871[3], there is a section devoted to "Treasurer of Symmes Township Hamilton County, O. in account with said Township for School Funds" and receipts include funds received from Hamilton

County Auditor George A. Larue for prolonging schools and "School House and Contingent Fund." Six districts are listed as well as a separate fund for Colored Schools. While it is not known for certain that individuals listed in this book as receiving a certain amount each month were actually teachers in our school, it would seem logical that James H. Holmes was also a teacher here, as he is listed on the same page in the same district as Frank Cunningham and W. P. O'Hara and he was active in the Sunday School, being the assistant Sunday School Superintendent at that time.

The following two programs which were contributed by Kate Kinney (Mrs. Ennes) Dawson of Loveland should be of interest to many people as they will bring to memory the names of many forgotten neighbors who were children in our village.

Programme of the Exhibition, Grand Valley School,

Friday Evening, June 18, 1875 at 8 P.M.

Song ....Do The Right
Recitations:
Lines for an exhibition...........................Ellen Ruff
Human Progress ....James Walsh
The Little Roan Colt......................Tommy Gallagher
The Peasant Girl........................Gladys Compton
Instrumental Music:
Dialogue ....The Little Children
   Smith Queal, Mamie Walsh, Lillie Buckingham, Maggie Walsh
Recitations:
The Thunder Storm........................Tracy Windsor
Do Thy Little — Do It Well....................Lucy Mount
The Light At Home........................Emma Vosburg
The Teachers Dream.........................Kate Kinney
Song ....Golden Gleams
Dialogue ....The Sincere Mourners
   Cora Ludlow, Hattie Bush, Ida Tullis
Recitations:
Labor ....Alvin Buckingham
The Dying Soldier...........................Lillie Radcliffe
The Leap For Life.............................Walter Price
Liberty and Independence.................Effie Buckingham
Instrumental Music:
Dialogue ....Eight O'clock
   Hattie Bush, Aphia Locke
Song ....Whisper, Sister, Whisper
   Ida Tullis and Cora Ludlow
Dialogue, 2 Scenes.........Boarding School Accomplishments:
Mr. Granville, Charles Kizer   Miss Bettie, Mary Radcliffe
Mr. Hopeful, Harold Longley   Miss Martha, Maggie Kizer

Recitations:
I'll be a Man..................................Morris Locke
Sheridan's Ride...............................Hattie Bush
Training Time................................Aphia Locke
The Young Patriot...........................Smith Queal
Instrumental Music:
Dialogue ....The Colonial Band
    Maggie Kinney, Mary Radcliffe, Temperance Mounce,
    Ida Tullis, Cora Ludlow, Sallie Hoffman, Kate Kinney,
    Tillie Compton, Ellen Ruff, Maggie Kizer, Lillie Radcliffe, Emma Vosburg, Effie Buckingham.
Song ....What Shall The Harvest Be?
Recitations:
The Polish Boy.............................Maggie Kinney
Fashion Now-A-Days........................Maggie Kizer
The Charge At Valley Maloy..........Raymond Cunningham
Stand Beside The Banner...................Sallie Hoffman
Song ....He's Got Money, Too
    Maggie Kizer
Dialogue, 3 scenes.....................Caratach and Hengo
    Caratach, General of the Britons........George Beard
    Hengo, a brave boy, nephew to Caratach
    ....Millard Vosburg
    Macer, a Roman Officer...................John Beard
    Judas, a Roman Corporal.............Harold Longley
    Roman Soldiers.........Walter Price and Chas. Kizer
Instrumental Music
Dialogue ....Blue Beard
Blue Beard, Charles Kizer   Lady Emiline, Sallie Hoffman
Lord Alphonse, Millard Vosburg   Lady Anne, Effie Buckingham
Lord Orlando, Harold Longley   Lady Eleanora, Maggie Kinney
Song ....Homeless Tonight
    Sallie Hoffman and Lillie Longley
Valedictory ....Miss Eva Dial
    Admission 15 cts.   Children 10 cts.

ENTERTAINMENT
Given by
THE GRAND VALLEY SCHOOLS
Friday Evening, June 8, 1877

Part One

Morning Chorus ....School
Salutatory ....Miss Katie Kinney
Address on Education................Mr. Frederick D. Peer
Declamations:
Don't Push a Man When He is Going Down Hill..John McClean
Hang Up Baby's Stocking...................Dovie Whitelock

Little Dot ....Ada Clark
Pinkie Winkies Mamma..................Belle Cunningham
Dialogue ....Boys Rights
  Carter Cunningham, Harry Clark, Ennis Price, Harry Savacool
Song ....Have Courage My Boy To Say No
     Tableau ....Temptation
Dialogue—Pride.....Lillie Buckingham and Alma Cunningham
Composition—Failure in Life....................Mary Hocter
Dialogue—What Little Girls Are Good For
  ....Mamie Walsh and others
Discussion—At Our House.....Eva McClean and Willie Kinney
     Declamations:
Benny...Lou Anna Radcliffe   Evening...Ettie Cunningham
Tom Twist..............................Thomas Gallagher
Dialogue—Shopping....Rena Longley, Smith Queal and others
     Tableau ....Boating
     Lord Dundrearys Visit
Belle Elwood, Katie Kinney   Gordon Elwood, John Kinney
Lillie Ashton, Maggie Kinney   Lord Dundreary, Willie Faul

     Part Two
     Declamations
Why a Dog's Nose is Cold................Alma Cunningham
Little Contrary.......................Blanche Cunningham
Song: Come Come to the Greenwood.................School
     Jack and the Beanstalk
Mrs. Twaddle, Katie Kinney   Horridhead, Walter Price
Helpalong, Hattie Bush   Scared to Death, Ella Ruff
Jack ....John Kinney
Dialogue—Boobeard......Eddie Bush and Lou Anna Radcliffe
Music ....Instrumental
     Tableau ....The Three Graces
Dialogue—The Little Tramp.........Tracy Windsor, L. Queal
     and Thomas Gallagher
     Witches in the Cream
Mrs. Churndasher, Ella Ruff   Geo. Gaylord, Walter Price
Miss Pickspider, Maggie Kizer   Harry Holystone, Willie Faul
Clementina, Cora Ludlow   Hezekiah Rackofbones, John Kinney
Duett—The Gypsy Countess..Mr. Charles and Miss Maggie Kizer
Recitation—The Wreck of the Hesperus............Hattie Bush
     Army and Navy Tableau
     Appearances are Deceitful
Oscar, T. Gallagher   Bootblack, O. Cunningham
Old Gent, W. Faul   Policeman, James Walsh
Fop, W. Glazier   Old Lady, Ella Ruff
     Valedictory, Lillie Fry

1. *Liberty Hall.* Dec. 1, 1811.
2. On deed held by Ohio Gravel Co.
3. Ledger book in possession of Mrs. Edith Knicely.

1890—Top Row: Tootsie Morris, Bertha Connett, Sarah Southworth, Belle Hodges, Unidentified, Maggie Harbor, Nat Green, Walter Mills, Henry Pinkvoss, Orville Sater, teacher, Lucien Cunningham.
3rd Row: Unidentified, Hattie Smith, Ralph Walton, Hattie Walton, Alice Cisco, Blanche Stewart, Charles Stewart, ——— Brown, ——— Brown, ——— Smith, Louis Walton, William Walton, Unidentified, Unidentified.
2nd Row: John Green, Anna Morris, Grace Kinney, Flora Robinson, Harold Fletcher, Charles Drake, William Price, Harry Cordes, Mamie Williams, Clarence Hartzell, Rolf Pinkvoss, W. Price, Nib Snyder, Stevie Detrick, ——— Snyder, Harry Cunningham.
1st Row: Elizabeth Marsh, Florence Cunningham, Clara Cordes, Fannie Edsall, Unidentified, Nellie Tittle, Anna Thompson.

1895-1896—Back Row: Mr. Jas. McGohan, teacher; George Williams, Rolf Pinkvoss, Alfred Buckingham, Flora Robinson, Fannie Edsall, Bell Hodges, Fannie Cullom, Melvina Prather, Mary Stewart.
1st Row: Eddie Prather, William Price, Clarence Hartzell, Henry Pinkvoss, John Green, Lillie Peteler, Elizabeth Marsh, Norman Little, Nellie Tittle, Florence Fletcher, Lillian Drake, Nellie Weber, Edna Thompson.
Kneeling: Charles Drake, Stanley Williams, Melville Little, Ralph Walton, Morris Walton, Harold Walton.

1898—Top Row: James McGohan, teacher.
4th Row: Mrs. Emma Quayle, music teacher, Grace Kinney, Laura Hartzell, Fannie Edsall, Sarah Southworth, Erma Marsh, Flora Robinson, Lela Marsh, teacher, Lorena Colthar, Pearl Hodges, Rolf Pinkvoss, Lillie Compton.
3rd Row: Agnes Cunningham, Lillie Peteler, Anna Peteler, May King, Clara Cordes, Mabel Heddleston, Florence Fletcher, Bell Hodges, ——— Cunningham, Elizabeth Marsh, Nellie Weber, Edna Thompson, Fannie Cullom, Lillian Drake, Melvina Prather, Mary Stewart, Nellie Tittle.
2nd Row: Julia Worsham, ——— Smith, William Price, Henry Pinkvoss, Clarence Hartzell, Harold Fltcher, Melville Little, William Walton, Oren Compton.
1st Row: Lida Walton, Julia Fletcher, Elsie Peterler, Orville Thompson, Norman Little, Raymond Fox, Elmer Cunningham, Harold Walton, Morris Walton, Hugh King.

About 1909 — Upper Room.
Top Row: Helen Wiley, Roma Buckingham, Mabel Brunner.
4th Row: ——— Ellis, Clara Bryant, Edith McAllister, ——— Ellis, Helen Waits, Gladys Ellis.
3rd Row: Mr. Thompson, teacher, Unidentified, Carl Ellis, Clifford Robinson, Bryan Brunner, Tom Hodges.
2nd Row: Wade Ellis, Clarence Brunner, Bernard Benken, Edwin Ellis, Earl Jones, Arch Cochran, Clifford Boyd, Clarence Fletcher.
1st Row: Harold Wiley, Lizzie Mintkenbaugh, Hallie Little.

1911-1912 — Lower Room.
Top Row: Florence Fletcher, teacher, Gus Benken, John Winkler, Chris Cochran, Henry Mintkenbaugh, Ted Peckenpagh, Anna Fox, Ariel Walton.
2nd Row: Gladys Worsham, Emily Case, Alice May Lewis, Elsa Applegate, Ethel Fletcher, Ruth Peckenpaugh, Edith Youngblutt, Eva Cochran, Ruth Matthews, Ray Hughes, Orville Hughes.
1st Row: James Robinson, Harry Winkler, Arthur Daughters, Harry Robinson, John Queal, Floyd Cordes, Carl Fletcher, Leroy Fox, Joseph Frazier, Russell Frazier.

1916-1917 — Upper Room.
Top Row: Leroy Fox, Edward Benken, William Richey, Harry Robinson, Floyd Cordes.
2nd Row: Anna Fox, Unidentified, Gladys Worsham.
1st Row: Laura Waits, Ethel Fletcher, Emily Case, Emma Mintkenbaugh, Dorothy Haller, Mary Barrere, Lillie Mintkenbaugh, Eva Cochran, Edith Youngblutt.

1916 — Lower Room.
Top Row: Ruth Matthews, Hilda Cochran, Zella Cochran, Ella Mae Knicely, teacher, Edna Mintkenbaugh, Mabel Youngblutt, Dorothy Frazier.
2nd Row: Audrey Waits, Edna Ward, Edna Benken, Ella Mae Waits, Carrie Anderson, Gladys Hutchinson, Velma Faul, Medell Prather, Unidentified, Alice Fox, Unidentified.
1st Row: John Robinson, Charles Anderson, Bill Fischer, Russell Peckenpaugh, John Queal, Unidentified, Unidentified, Unidentified, Unidentified.

1922-1923 — Upper Room.
Top Row: John Robinson, Dick Frazier, Genevieve Robinson, Hester Bennett.
3rd Row: Ted Hathman, Blanche Robinson.
2nd Row: Audrey Waits, Edna Benken, Carrie Anderson, Hazel Lewis, Mr. Porter Hancock, teacher.
1st Row: Marguerite Chalfant, Velma Faul, Charles Anderson, Wilbur Bauer, Henrietta Fischer.

1922-1923 — Lower Room.
Top Row: Kenneth Knicely, Herbert Jones, Charles Bauer, Medell Prather.
3rd Row: Permelia Anderson, Frank Waits.
2nd Row: Lilly May Story, Patsy Bennett, Matilda Robinson, Elsie Frazier, Ethlyn Stivers, teacher.
1st Row: Herman Benken, Mildred Anderson, Marjorie Anderson, Ruby Richey, Edward Anderson, John Benker, Henry Pinkvoss, Turner Laudeman, Rita Meyers

1925-1926 — Upper Room.
Top Row: Herbert Jones, Clarence Cox, Kenneth Knicely, John Benken.
5th Row: Claude Moore, Frank Waits, Henry Pinkvoss.
4th Row: Paul Linke, David Meyer.
3rd Row: Elsie Frazier, Ruth Moore, Lucille Ladd, Grace Moore.
2nd Row: Unidentified, Turner Laudeman.
1st Row: Eddie Anderson, Frances Gant, Ruby Richey, ——— Ladd, Helen Ausman, Permelia Anderson, Marguerite Chalfant.

1925-1926 — Lower Room.
Top Row: Henry Robinson.
4th Row: Herman Benken, Walter Moore, Charles Ausman, Unidentified, Mildred Anderson, Rita Meyers.
3rd Row: Howard Little, Charles Quinn, Donald Richey, Earl Gant.
2nd Row: Ruby Frazier, Anna Marie Brunner, Bedah Henize, teacher.
1st Row: Bill Laudeman, Horatio Flint, Eleanor Quinn, Velma Chalfant, Marjorie Anderson, Unidentified, Virgina Meyers.

1940 — Upper Room.
Top Row: Charles Rahn, Bob Quayle, ———— Martin, ———— Thornhill, Earl Howell, Jr., ———— Martin, Mosier King, Kenneth Singleton.
3rd Row: Lowell Boggs, Eileen Ward, Carolyn Dority, ———— DeGraw, Jean Dority, Mary Jane Frank, Jean Anderson, Unidentified, Robert Greene, teacher.
2nd Row: Paul Moore. Doris Oligee, Helen Gant, ———— Martin, ———— Martin, Margaret Greene, ———— Martin, Eleanor Gant, Lillian Reeder, Mary Bell Thornhill.
1st Row: Henry Sites, Roland Frank, Luther Boggs, Allan Fry, ———— DeGraw, Bill Oligee, Ray Singleton, Owen White.

1940 — Lower Room.
Top Row: Unidentified, Unidentified, ———— Boggs, Unidentified, Harley Singleton, Gordon Coyle, Tom Quayle, Evelyn Wells, Beverly Coats.
3rd Row: Unidentified, Louise Coats, Gloria Quinn, Juanita Ward, Phyllis Ward, Audrey Martin, Norma Reeder, Mary Jane Frankenburg, John Sexton, Ada Kelly, teacher.
2nd Row: Marjorie Anderson, Unidentified, Joyce Singleton, Anna Belle Sexton, Unidentified, James Quinn, Dorothy Wells, Mary L. Rahn, Ruby Greene, Unidentified, Unidentified.
1st Row: Paul White, Eugene White, Harold Caldwell, Charles Ferguson, Carl Frank, Rolf Dority, Glenn Howell.

1947 — Upper Room.
Top Row: Ken Miller, Rolf Dority.
3rd Row: Patricia Westerkamm, Jeanette Westerkamm, Dorothy Wells, Beverly Coats, Marjorie Anderson, Catherine Greene, Mabel Price.
2nd Row: James Quinn, Bill Hillard, Frances Johnson, Herbert Hillard, Dick Weaver.
1st Row: Eugene White, John Jones, Marva Lee Nibert, Evelyn Hillard, Don Freeman, Allan Wogenstahl, Donald Curless, Bill Nibert, Daniel Ward, John Coats, Paul White, Mr. Roy Eltzroth, teacher.

Lower Room — 1947.
Top Row: Mrs. Eltzroth, teacher.
4th Row: Betty Hicks, Charlene Bernart, Geraldine McClain, Frances Langford, Jeanne Skor, Harold Curless, Earl Jones.
3rd Row: Charles Williams, Jack Westerkamm, Herbert Jones, Carol Hicks, Robert Miller, Bob Hillard.
2nd Row: Carold Wogenstahl, Nancie Ferguson, John Anderson, Janice Langford, Irene Dunn, Marlene Miller, Katherine Turner.
1st Row: Philip Ferguson, Pierce Jones, Unidentified, Harry Carter, Georganne Dunn, Helen Bernart, Gary Jones, Donald Weaver, Christi Westerkamm, David Weaver.

Chapter VII

TWO MORE WARS — 1917 TO PRESENT

The comparative tranquility of the foregoing scenes was to be upset by the occurrence of two great wars, the advent of the automobile, the factory system, and indeed shows how the tremendous evolution of American life swept with it such outlying communties as Camp Dennison. Having the constant advantages of rapid communication and transportation which are the hallmarks of our century, Camp Dennison escaped the fate of becoming "provincial" as did some of our European sisters, developing their own cultural idiom, dialect and customs.

Camp Dennison's townspeople formerly met at church and church functions, and produced their own entertainment in the form of quilting parties or minstrel shows. Occasionally neighbors living as far as two or three miles away joined in these celebrations, and Milford boasted an "orchestra" which furnished music for the little commencements of six or seven school children.

To the first call of war the following men responded, as shown on a roll of honor hanging in the rear of the Methodist church: Louis Adams, Gerald Barrere, Harold Barrere, George Bauer, William Benken, Clifford Boyd, Homer Boyd, Howard

Tennis court about 1925. Audrey Waits, John Robinson, Lloyd Lewis, Chris Cochran and Kenneth Knicely.

Brown, Bryan Brunner, Charles Brunner, Archie Cochran, James Cochran (died of flu while in service), Joseph Gordon, Fred Grau, Henry Mintkenbaugh, Joseph Mintkenbaugh, J. Matson Quayle, Archie Reed, Clifford Robinson, and Minor Wiley.

Again in 1941 the same problems were dealt with in the same way. Blue stars were hung in the windows of homes which lent their young men to the war effort. One, Lester Ward, was killed in an accident in Italy. The others were fortunate enough to return home. Every town in the nation then had its public placard of names of people in service and in Camp Dennison this board stood by the Post Office. The names of those who served during World War II and the ones who have been in the service since then follows: Charles Anderson, Lawrence Anderson, Leroy Brumagen, Earl Carter, Howard Clark, John Cosby, Susie Cosby, Thomas Cox, Frederic Dunn, Albert Edwards, Elmer Elder, Roy Elder, Gilbert Elstun, Charles Ferguson, Earl Ferguson, Geneva Ferguson, Ellery Frankenburg, Dorothy Frazier, Richard Frazier, Allan Fry, Ted Hathman, William Hillard, Kenneth Knicely, John Krome, Everett Leadmon, Richard Lewis, Howard Little, Orville McClain, Edward Martin, James Martin, Joseph Martin, William Oligee, Henry F. Pinkvoss, Charles Rahn, Jacob Reichert, Duane Sewell, Harley Singleton, Kenneth Singleton, Raymond Singleton, William Singleton, John Stewart, Richard Tyler, Lester Ward, David Weaver, Richard Weaver, Robert Wells, Eugene White, Paul White and William White.

During the crisis the Ladies' Auxiliary of the Red Cross met regularly at the school house preparing surgical dressings, hospital supplies, robes and toilet kits for the boys.

Electric Service

E. B. Bentley, Assistant Manager, Electric Sales Department of the Cincinnati Gas and Electric Company, has supplied us with the following information from that Company's files:

"On September 1, 1919, the Cincinnati, Milford and Blanchester Traction Company filed with the Public Utilities Commission of Ohio a schedule of rates and charges for extending electric service lines to Milford, Newtown, Newtonsville, Terrace Park and the Plainville districts. Four years later, December 1, 1923, this company made a supplement to the first filing to include Camp Dennison, Miamiville, Blanchester and the areas adjacent to them.

"The main line to the Camp Dennison - Miamiville area was then built by the C. M. & B. Traction Company with the customers furnishing the poles at their expense and the Traction Company, the wires, cross arms, insulators and transformers. For this construction the original subscribers agreed to pay the sum of $2000. The individual connection to the line for each customer was to be paid for in advance by the customer and then refunded to the customer by the C. M. & B. Traction Company in the form of a 5% discount on the monthly bills. The refund did not cover labor, but only material.

"The rate charged for electricity was 10¢ per KwHr. with a cash discount of 5% if paid within ten days.

"The Cincinnati, Milford and Blanchester Traction Company was then referred to as the 'Kroger Line' and its President in 1923 was Mr. I. W. Pettengill, son-in-law of Mr. (Bernard) Kroger. The electric power was furnished by a power plant located in Milford and prior to the building of the Camp Dennison - Miamiville line, service was always discontinued at midnight.

"About the time the Camp Dennison line was built or shortly thereafter, the 'Kroger Line' was acquired by a Mr. Al G. Van Ness who also bought the Cincinnati, Georgetown and Portsmouth Traction line. He discontinued the operation of the C. M. & B. Traction service and combined the electric service part of the 'Kroger Line' with other lines into the Southwestern Ohio Power Company. He also found it cheaper and more advantageous to buy energy from the Union Gas and Electric Company (later The Cincinnati Gas & Electric Company) and discontinued the operation of the Milford power plant. This was the beginning of twenty-four hour service in this area.

"In 1926 Mr. Van Ness sold the Southwestern Ohio Power Company to the Columbia Gas & Electric Corporation, and in 1935 the Southwestern Ohio Power Company was merged with the Union Gas & Electric Company to form The Cincinnati Gas & Electric Company which now serves this area.

"It was only about six years ago that the last refunds were made on the original customers' deposits for line extensions. It is interesting to note that since the original line was built, the cost of electricity per KwHr. has dropped to about one-third the original cost which was 10¢ in 1923 and in 1954 averaged about 3.37¢."[1]

Albert D. Flint, son-in-law of Horatio Buckingham, promoted the building of the line to Camp Dennison and Miamiville. Mr. Flint, being an electrician, wired most of the houses in both villages. He was assisted by Clifford (Sam) Jackson.

4-H Clubs

Young girls formed a 4-H Club in 1924, their aim in some years being sewing, in others, cooking. One program, for the year 1943-44 shows an interesting variety of monthly projects:

October—Hallowe'en Party (Boy Scouts invited)
November—Play (Minstrel performed in January)
December—Christmas Party (at Mrs. Genevieve Greene's house)
January—Roller Rink
February—Valentine Party (Square Dance)
April—Hay Ride
May—Hike and lunch
June—Coney Island
July—Camp
August—Trolley tour of Cincinnati
September—County Fair

The 4-H Clubs generally met every two weeks, either in

homes of members or at the school house. The girls also assisted the various charities, the war effort, and conducted Sunday School upon occasion.

Sewing and cooking club leaders were:

1924—Mrs. Susie Buckingham; 1925 to 1930—Mrs. Chas. Ausman; 1934—Violet Wartnaby; 1940—Ruth Menke; 1941 and 1942—Mrs. C. W. Rahn; 1942 to 1944—Mrs. Elmer Kindt: 1944—Mrs. William Gant; 1945—Mrs. Bertha Oligee; 1945—Ruby Wilson.

There was another girls' 4-H club around 1917, with Mrs. Susie Buckingham in charge, but no written records of it can be found.

In 1927, a boys' 4-H Club devoted to gardening, under the leadership of Joe Meyer, was active. It lasted four years.

Carl Bibee, Agricultural Agent and 4-H Club advisor organized both boys' and girls' clubs and was succeeded by Clinton Caldwell, Ingram and William Tyree.[2]

Boy Scouts

The Boy Scouts of America, Troop No. 506, was active in Camp Dennison 1942 to 1945. They constructed a club house on property belonging to Dr. R. D. Pinkvoss on Galbraith Road in 1943. Allan Fry was Scout Leader until he went into the service in 1944 and Wilbur Fletcher carried on in his place until he returned from the Army. Allan took over then for a short time and later Herbert Wardlow was leader for a short time. The troop disbanded when the school building was dismantled as they had no meeting place. Milton Freeman, Glenn Howell and Charles Rahn were Assistant Leaders at different times.

Water Supply

According to the County Engineer's Office in the Hamilton County Courthouse, water lines connecting with Cincinnati, through Indian Hill, were laid along Route 126 in 1930. Indian Hill established its own water station in Camp Dennison in the winter of 1949 and since that time we have been supplied from their wells.

Camp Ross

This target ground for the 147th Infantry of the Ohio National Guard is located in the area formerly excavated by the Granite Improvement Co. It was formerly leased by the Citizens Military Finance Committee of Cincinnati, headed by General P. Lincoln Mitchell, from the Pennsylvania Railroad. Title to the property was eventually acquired by the Committee in the name of the Central Trust Co., which in 1948 conveyed it to the State of Ohio in consideration of $1.00. It is under control of the Adjutant General's Department. Its barracks were razed by fire some years ago and were not rebuilt.

Camp Dennison Concrete Block Co.

Concrete blocks and similar masonry products are being built by the Camp Dennison Concrete Block Company on a lot adjacent to the abandoned schoolhouse. Mr. John G. Ashby is president of the concern and first started operations at the corner of Daniels and Jackson Streets. Mr. Ashby acquired the business of the Miami Brikcrete Co. in December 1950 and moved to his present location. The company employs five men.

Filling Station

The Sohio Filling Station on Route 126 is now owned and operated by Mr. Morris Walton. It was formerly operated by Harry Carter, among others, and was built by Mr. and Mrs. Louis Walton, in 1932.

The Ohio Gravel Company

The Ohio Gravel Company opened in Camp Dennison in 1946. It now owns the entire area between the Highway and the river for two miles north of Zumstein's Lane to the Jennie B. Queal farm now owned by Mr. Joseph Faul. A prize fossil, an intact mammoth tusk ten feet long, was unearthed at a depth of twenty-five feet during their digging here. It was presented to the Cincinnati Natural History Musuem, where curators have pronounced it 10,000 to 35,000 years old. The tusk was carried to this area by the Wisconsin Glacier.

A portion of a mammoth tusk, three feet long, found March, 1955, in this area, has (as well as we can estimate) the same history. Mr. Morgan of Mt. Carmel secured this fossil for the Trailside Museum in Burnet Woods.

The Ohio Gravel Company purchased the old schoolhouse and acreage in 1952.

THE WALDSMITH HOME
State Shrine of the Daughters of the American Revolution

Mrs. Ramona Kaiser Bradley was first chairman when the restoration of the home of Christian Waldsmith began. The property, with a gift of money, was given to the group by Mr. and Mrs. Chester Kroger. Robert Kennedy was the architect appointed to supervise the work. After the death of Mr. Kroger, Mrs. Kroger donated the brick walk and the porch floor in memory of her husband. The Second World War made rapid progress of the work impossible, but the building was dedicated and opened to the public October 23, 1952. Since then the groups in charge have collected bits of early Americana and furnishings that were originally used by Christian Waldsmith and his family.

Plaque on Waldsmith Museum.   Photo by Rob Paris.

In the kitchen are six original chairs, a ladder-back rocker, a safe with six perforated tin panels, wooden pitchfork, candle molds, a cookie press, coffee mill and such examples of ancient cooking ware as fireplace toasters, griddles and Dutch ovens. The main architectural feature of the kitchen is the giant fireplace.

In the front room are portraits of Rebecca West Kugler, John Kugler, James Given and Sarah Waldsmith Given.

Upstairs are the paraphernalia of pioneer sleeping comfort: Beds made of straw mattresses upon rope "springs," some very old quilts, and the bedwarmers that lessened the suffering of the sleepy person who was faced with the prospect of cold linen sheets . . . and nothing can seem as cold as linen in mid-winter!

Some visitors remark that the maternity bed shown here seems to be an extraneous piece of furniture. The answer is, that in the days of large families, and quite often with multiple households living under the same roof, such equipment was in nearly constant use.

There is a collection of earthenware familiar to houses not equipped with plumbing, including a candle stand with perforated shade that probably served as a night lamp.

The museum is open to the public on Sunday afternoons during the Summer months, and a staff of volunteers is always on hand to describe the oddities to visitors.

Recent Growth

In the late 1940's, Ohio Homes, Inc. purchased a tract of land on the southwest corner of Camp and Lincoln Streets and began constructing 16 houses. Later they built 21 houses on Lincoln Road east of the store and 11 houses west of the church on Jackson, which increased our population by about 200 people.

Considerable excitement ensued in 1954 when Hamilton County attempted to construct a garbage incinerator across the road from the museum. A group of dauntless civic leaders and

D.A.R. officials took prompt action to protest this desecration, and in their zeal even appeared at a meeting that was not actually "public" . . . nevertheless they met face to face with the chief protagonists of the project, and so the committeemen found themselves in the middle of a veritable battleground that day, and suspended the meeting without accomplishing anything. The first bids on the project lapsed, however, before any building was undertaken.

BIOGRAPHICAL SKETCHES OF FAMILIES WHO HAVE MOVED INTO CAMP DENNISON SINCE 1917

Charles and Louise AUSMAN came here in 1924 from Milford, Ohio — moved to New Richmond, Ohio and are now living in Maineville, Ohio. Mr. Ausman was a telegraph operator for the Pennsylvania Railroad. Mrs. Ausman was active in the church, teaching a class for several years, and was leader of the girls' 4-H sewing club. Of their children, Helen is married to Don Sanders, a mortician at Port Clinton, Ohio, and has no children. Charles married Estelle Kipp and has three children, Christine, Linda and Charles. They live in Cheviot, Ohio. Alice is married to Ernie Irwin and lives at Kings Mills, Ohio. They have three children, Susan, Terry Lee and Jennie Lee. Paul, who was born in Maineville, is married to Wanda Ellis.[3]

Charles CHALFONT and his wife, who was the sister of Joseph Faul, moved here about 1920 into House No. 54 (Illus. 49). They had three daughters, May Having who lives in Perintown, Ohio, Marguerite Newport who lives in Oroville, California, and Velma Jenkins who lives in Cincinnati. Mrs. Chalfont died in 1948.[4]

Mr. and Mrs. Roy ELTZROTH began teaching in our school in 1944. Since his wife's death in 1952, Mr. Eltzroth has built a new home on Galbraith Road near Camp, and he is now Principal of the Branch Hill, Ohio, school.[5]

Mr. and Mrs. Leo FALGNER bought the Haffenbradl farm about 1919. They have both died since living here. There were six children: Charles, who was married before they moved here; William, Nelle, Agnes, Mary and Leonora. Leonora died a few years after coming to Camp Dennison and Agnes died in 1955. They sold their farm to Excello Paper Co. in 1955 and have bought a home in Milford.[6]

Henry and Ida Mae FRANKENBERG and their family lived here from 1932 to 1942 on the Paxton farm. They are now living in Xenia, Ohio. They have four children. Alberta is married to William Kuhnell, lives in Blanchester, Ohio and has three children. Mary Jane lives in Painesville, Ohio and has one child. Ellery is married to Anita Lassiter and has two children. They live in Madeira, Ohio. Mildred was married to John Fuller and has two children. Mildred played the piano in the church.[7]

Robert GREENE came here as a teacher in 1935. He and Mrs. Genevieve Greene have three daughters: Margaret, who is married to Charles Rahn; Ruby who lives with her mother in Madeira, Ohio where they moved in 1952; and Catherine, who was married to Robert Burroughs in April 1956 and who lives in Camp Dennison. The Greene family was active in the church and Sunday School until they moved.[8]

Mr. and Mrs. Harry E. GANT moved here in 1926 when they bought the Queal farm south of the village. Mrs. Gant and four of the children still live here: Bill who is married to Velma Faul; Frances who has one son, John Kirschner; Evelyn; and Helen who is married to Frank Lohr and has three children. The other children are: Edward (Eddie) who is married to Sara Wycoff, has two daughters and lives in Mt. Washington, Cincinnati, Ohio; Albert who married Hazel Stricker, and lives in West Virginia; Earl (Fritz) who is married to Fay Berger, has one child, and lives in Kenwood, Cincinnati, Ohio; and Eleanor who is married to Ralph Lay, has two children and lives in Milford.[9]

Mrs. Mary HILLARD and five of her children moved here in January 1946, when they bought the house on Route 126 where they are living at the present time. One daughter Ethel is married to Lynn Moore; Evelyn, Herbert and Robert are living at home and William is in the Navy.[10]

Earl and Leonora HOWELL moved to the village in 1928. They first lived in House No. 154 on the corner of Jackson and Camp Roads. Later they bought the old Price home where they are living at the present time. Earl is a Symmes Township trustee and a trustee of the Methodist Church. They have two sons — Earl Jr. (Jake) lives at home and Glenn is married to Mary Breidenstein and they have a small son. Glenn and Mary live in the building next to his parents.[11]

Jennie and Elmer KINDT built their house on Route 126 and moved here from Miamiville, Ohio in 1936. Elmer, an Indian Hill Village Ranger, died in 1944, and Jennie later married James MORRIS. She was always a leader in the church and community affairs, being president of the Woman's Society and leader of 4-H Clubs, chairman of Red Cross Sewing and Canning during the World War II. She always helped to solicit for the Red Cross and Community Chest and was willing to help in any cause. Jim Morris was Sunday School Superintendent for a couple of years. They moved to Lockland, Ohio, and since have been divorced.[12]

Albert and Elsie LAUDEMAN lived here from 1922 to 1930. They had two sons, Turner and William. Turner and his wife live in Detroit, Michigan. They have four boys and one girl. Bill is married to Dorothy Arndt and lives in Milford. They have one girl and one boy.[13]

Mr. and Mrs. James LOCKWOOD live in House 47 on Lincoln Road. Mrs. Alfrieda Lockwood's first husband was Rudolph Bayer, son of Mrs. Sophie Bayer, and she moved here about 1926. She has one son, Theodore (Teddy) Bayer, who is married to Henrietta Klopp and lives in Madeira, Ohio. They have three children.[14]

Joseph and Elizabeth MARTIN moved into House No. 84

on Cunningham Road in 1940. They had nine children all of whom are married. Nannie Brunk, Hattie Setty, Dorothy Dunlap, Norma Sewell, Ernestine Holden, Sam, Amos, Charles and James. Mrs. Martin died in the spring of 1955. Mr. Martin still lives in the house on Cunningham Road and James and his wife and son live in one of Mrs. Knicely's apartments. One grandchild, Paul Holden, is married to Catherine Turner and lives in the village. Two of Mrs. Martin's nephews also live here; George Malott and his wife and two children, and Leroy Malott and his wife and two children. Mrs. Martin was active in the Methodist Church and five of her grandchildren, the children of Nannie Brunk, joined church the same time their grandmother did.[15]

Clark C. and Emma A. MYERS bought the farm on Highway 126 in 1917. John, Grant and Stanley were married and had families at that time and never lived here, but the following children moved here with the family: Wilber who has been very active in the Methodist church, having been Sunday School Superintendent for several years and a member of the Board of Trustees of the church for many years; Etna who was married to Bill Jentz and who died in May 1956; Finley who lives at home; Lillian who returned home from Washington, D. C. to keep house for the family after their mother died and who died in 1944; and Pauline who is employed at the Bethesda Hospital. The Myers farm has now been sold to the Ohio Gravel Co. and the family has bought the Fry home (House 110) on Lincoln Road.[16]

The Charles QUINN family moved to the community in 1924 when they bought the house on Lincoln Road from Frank Fischer who moved away. Their three daugthers are married and live in the village: Eleanor is married to Charles Reeder; Dorothy is married to Irvin Miller and has two daughters, Judy and Joan, and one son, Thomas; and Gloria is married to Francis Drusell and has two children, Vickie and Michael. Charles Quinn Jr. lives at home and James is married to Evelyn Field and has one daughter, Catherine Marie.[17]

Mr. and Mrs. Walter RABE moved here in 1938 from Cincinnati to take care of her mother, Mrs. Sophie Bayer. They later bought the house on Lincoln Road (House 19) which Mrs. Bayer had built in 1933. Mr. and Mrs. Rabe have two married sons but they have never lived in our village.[18]

Mr. and Mrs. Russell ROBE, while not living in the village, are considered as belonging to us as they and their children, Marilyn and Carl, are active in the church and Mr. Robe is a Trustee. They were transferred from South Charleston, Ohio, in 1944, to the Kroger farm which Mr. Robe supervises.[19]

John Ringenberger served in one of the three months' enlistments at Camp Dennison during the Civil War. He was born in Germany, as were the parents of his wife. Their only daughter, Elizabeth, married August RAHN, a German immigrant, who later operated the Rahn Bakery on Cincinnati's Eastern Avenue in the 1890's. They moved to Camp Dennison in 1920 and lived the rest of their lives in the house south of the Waldsmith Museum. Three of their seven children now live in Camp Dennison: Elsie, Carrie and C. Wesley.

Elsie and her husband, Henry PITSER, moved into their home on Lincoln Road in 1922. Mr. Pitser was employed at LeBlond's in Hyde Park for 30 years.[20]

Carrie Rahn is the wife of Herman HALLER and is an accomplished pianist. The Hallers first came here in 1913 to operate the farm owned by his uncle, Henry F. Pinkvoss. For the past several years they have made their home with their daughter, Dorothea Dority, a widow, who has four children: Jean Schudel, a nurse who lives in Toledo and has one son; Carolyn; Rolf who is married to Norma Howell, lives above Milford and has two daughters; and Robert, member of the Cincinnati Police Force, who lives in Mt. Washington with his wife, Joyce Tolin, and two daughters.

C. Wesley Rahn now lives in the house formerly occupied by his parents. He has operated a barbecue on U. S. 50 in Milford for twenty-five years. He and his wife, Myrtle, have two children: Charles, who married Margaret Greene — they have four children; and Mary, wife of Glenn Sloan, symphony orchestra trombonist, who has two sons, Aaron and Marc.

George August Rahn and his wife moved here in 1948 in House No. 9 (Illus. 49). He died in 1955 and has one son in California. Mrs. "Gus" Rahn has now moved to Cincinnati.[20]

Mr. and Mrs. James RITCHIE lived on the Paxton farm for a good many years and are now living near Blanchester, Ohio. They had five children: William who lives in Cincinnati; Ruby who was injured in an automobile accident and who died when about 18; Donald; John; and Hobart.[21]

The Homer SINGLETON family moved to Camp Dennison from Kentucky in 1927. They first lived in House No. 7 on Route 126 and in 1931 purchased House No. 14 from Miss Bessie Thompson. They have five children, all of whom were baptized in the Methodist Church as well as Mrs. Flora Singleton herself. William is married to Gay Fuller and has three children. They live in Milford. Kenneth is married to Betty Pickelheimer and has three children. Raymond is in the service. He is not married. Harley lives at home. Joyce (Boots) was married to Gene Iles in the Camp Dennison Methodist Church. They have one little boy. Her husband is now in the service.[22]

The James STRONG family lived on Camargo Road near Kugler Mill Road and attended our Methodist church for about twelve years during the 1930's and 1940's. Mrs. Strong was a leader in the church, being Sunday School Superintendent at one time and president of the Ladies' Bible Class for eight years. They have two children: Mary Louise who is married to James Emerson and who has one son and one daughter, and James Albert who is married to Viola Brandenberg and who has one son and one daughter. The Strongs now live in Rossmoyne, Ohio.[23]

Mr. and Mrs. Vernon TAYLOR have resided in the Longley house (House 156) since 1949. They have a son Ronnie and a younger daughter Bonnie.[24]

William TURNER and his family moved here in 1935 when they bought the house on the corner of Kilgore and Jackson Streets (House 125). They have four children: Lillian DeWitt; Charles Reeder who is married to Eleanor Quinn; Norma Hardin who has four children; and Catherine Holden, who has one daughter. Charles, Norma and Catherine are still living in our village. Mrs. Turner died in May 1956.[25]

Mr. and Mrs. William WARD lived in the small Knicely house (House No. 11) from 1932 until 1954, when they moved to Cincinnati. They had six children. Martha and Eileen married Robert and James Kelly, brothers, and they live in Seattle, Washington; Lester was killed in World War II; Juanita is married to Lou Dehner and lives in Los Angeles; Phyllis is married to Jack Clemons and lives in Mt. Repose, Ohio; and Daniel is still living at home. Opal Tyler, a daughter of Mr. Ward, lived with her husband, Richard TYLER, on Camp Road, for several years. They have one son, Rickie.[26]

Mr. and Mrs. Henry WEAVER moved into the Wartnaby house on Jackson and Kilgore Streets in 1944. They have since moved to their house on Ulrich Lane. Of their four children, Richard and David are in the Air Force, and Donald and Joyce are still at home.[27]

Mrs. Weaver's sister and her husband, Mr. and Mrs. Guy STINETTE, who lived in House No. 150 on Cunningham Road, moved away in October 1955. They have two children, Guy and Carol.

Mr. and Mrs. Louis WESTERKAMM moved here from Dent, Ohio, in 1941, and bought the property on the river at the end of Lincoln Road from Albert Wurster, an uncle, who was one of the old timers in the old Camp Superior down there. He is still living down by the river in a house back of the Westerkamms. The Westerkamms since 1946 have had a picnic grounds on their property, which they rent to groups by the day. They have five children: Louis Jr. who is married to Caroline Carter from Milford and who has one daughter Lori; Jeannette who is married to Richard Cain from Milford and who has one son, Richard Allen, and one daughter, Kim Susan; Patricia, John Bernard and Christi Ann who are at home.[28]

Mrs. Jeannetta WIGGINS actually moved to Camp Dennison in 1938 with her daughter Vivian. However, the Wiggins family homestead was on Galbraith Road west of Given Road and the family was well known and active here. The first representatives of the Wiggins (or Wiggans) family who settled here are buried in the Camp Dennison Cemetery. Mrs. Wiggins' husband, William J., was an officer of the Symmes Township Sunday School Convention for many years. Mr. and Mrs. Wiggins had two children: Vernon who lives in Florida, and Vivian who is married to Harry Montag and lives on Camp Road (House No. 140) where her mother was living at the time of her death in 1956.[29]

Negro Families Who Have Moved Here Since 1917

The CALDWELL family moved here in 1925. All of the children are now married and four of them still live in the village: (1) Ailene O'Banion, who has one son; (2) Woodruff, who has one boy; (3) Thomas, who has four children; (4) and Harold who has two children. (5) Mary Ellen Hughes has five children and lives on Camargo Road between Miamiville and Guinea, Ohio; (6) Thelma Davis lives in Madisonville, Cincinnati, and has two children; and (7) Helen Green lives in Milford. The son of Russell Caldwell, who died in 1941, also lives in Camp Dennison.[30]

Mr. and Mrs. Harley EDWARDS built their home on Lincoln Road in 1929 (House No. 21, Illus. 49). Mr. Edwards by his first marriage had four children: Albert, who lives in Cleveland, Ohio and has two boys; Kathryn Austin, Pittsburgh, Pennsylvania, three children; Consuelo Bryers, Cincinnati, two children; and Daisy Albright, Cleveland, Ohio, six children.[31]

Mr. and Mrs. Charles FERGUSON bought the Peckenpaugh house on Camp Road (House No. 138, Illus. 49) about 1925. In addition to their one daughter, Hazel, who died in infancy, their family included: (1) Edith Keels, who lives in Woodlawn, Ohio, and has two boys; (2) Clara Knight, Madisonville, Cincinnati, Ohio, one daughter; (3) John, who is married to Hester Bennett; (4) Charles, who also lives in Madisonville and has three boys; (5) Minnie Davis of Pittsburgh, Pennsylvania; (6) Harriet Walker, Cincinnati, has two girls; (7) Ruth Buggs, Cincinnati, two girls; (8) Florence Shelton, who is in Japan with her four daughters and husband who is a Captain in the service; (9) Earl, Cincinnati, two boys; (10) Geneva Bland who was a WAC in World War II and who has one boy and one girl; and (11) Willa Hawkins, Cincinnati, who has one daughter. Mr. Ferguson died in 1955.[32]

Mr. Clarence ELSTUN moved here to House No. 62 in 1946.

His son, Gilbert, now lives in House 134 on Washington St. and his stepson, Harry Hughes, is married to Matilda Robinson and lives on Route 126 (House No. 52).[33]

Mr. and Mrs. Booker T. HUNTER moved here in 1929 and in 1935 built the house on Lincoln Street where they now live. (House No. 102, Illus. 49).[34]

Orville and Catherine McCLAIN came here with their grandparents, Mr. and Mrs. Hathman, in 1937. Catherine has since married and is living away from here. Orville is married and lives in his grandparents' home (No. 86, Illus. 49). He and Mrs. McClain have seven daughters: Hazel, Cynthia, Patricia, Pamela, Yvonne, Andrea, and Kathleen.[35]

Henry and Carrie ROBINSON came to our village in 1920. They are the parents of ten children: Bessie Houston, Cincinnati, has three children; Stanley, Cincinnati; Genevieve Brockman, Cincinnati, one child; Ann (Blanche) Watts, two children; Fannie, Cincinnati; Henry, Loveland; and Matilda Hughes, Camp Dennison, one child. Matilda and her husband have a grocery store in Madisonville, Cincinnati, Ohio. One daughter, Myrtle Coats, is deceased, as are two babies who died in infancy.[36]

Mr. and Mrs. John WHITE came here around 1940 and operated the Miami Valley Inn until January 1956 when his nephew, Owen White, took over. Mr. and Mrs. White have one daughter Valerie and live in House No. 69 (Illus. 49).[37]

Mr. and Mrs. Perry WILLIAMS moved to our village in 1919. They had three children, Stanley, Commodore and Grace Williams WHITE. Stanley lives in Cincinnati and has two girls and one boy. Commodore married Ailene Caldwell and they had one son, Charles. Commodore is now deceased. Grace White had five children, and her one daughter, Gladys, was killed by an automobile while a child. William, Owen and Eugene still live in Camp Dennison, and William and Owen are both married and each has one child. Owen is now proprietor of the Miami Valley Inn. Paul, another son, lives in San Francisco. Grace, who is now Mrs. Strode, is living in Dayton, Ohio.[38]

Enos WILLIAMS moved here from West Virginia in 1942. He is married to Edith Carroll from Milford and has four children, Jacqueline, Carolyn, Lloyd and Enos Donald II. They live in House No. 87 on the main highway, at the corner of Campbell Street.[39]

1. E. B. Bentley, Asst. Manager, Electric Sales Department, Cincinnati Gas & Electric Co., Cincinnati, Ohio.
2. The Agricultural Extension Service, Greenhills, Ohio.
3. Source of information — Charles Ausman.
4. Source — Mrs. Joseph Faul.

5. Source — Roy Eltzroth.
6. Source — William Falgner.
7. Source — Ellery Frankenberg.
8. Source — Mrs. Genevieve Greene.
9. Source — William Gant.
10. Source — Mrs. Mary Hillard.
11. Source — Mrs. Earl Howell.
12. Source — Mrs. Jennie Morris.
13. Source — Mrs. Elsie Laudeman.
14. Source — Mrs. James Lockwood.
15. Source — Mrs. Nannie Brunk.
16. Source — Miss Pauline Myers.
17. Source — Mrs. Dorothy Miller.
18. Source — Mrs. Walter Rabe.
19. Source — Mrs. Russell Robe.
20. Source — Mrs. Glenn Sloan and Mrs. Elsie Pitser.
21. Source — Wilber Myers.
22. Source — Mrs. Flora Singleton.
23. Source — Mrs. James Strong.
24. Source — Mrs. Vernon Taylor.
25. Source — Mrs. John Hardin.
26. Source — Mrs. William Ward.
27. Source — Mrs. Henry Weaver.
28. Source — Mrs. Louis Westerkamm.
29. Source — Mrs. Vivian Montag.
30. Source — Thomas Caldwell.
31. Source — Harley Edwards.
32. Source — Mrs. John Ferguson.
33. Source — Gilbert Elstun.
34. Source — Booker T. Hunter.
35. Source — Orville McClain.
36. Source — Mrs. Carrie Robinson.
37. Source — John White.
38. Source — Mrs. Grace Strode.
39. Source — Enos Williams.

Chapter VIII

" . . . with each turn the houses, streets, river, and gardens of the town below came closer and grew more distinct. Soon I could distinguish the roofs and pick out the familiar ones; soon, too, I could count the windows . . . and while childhood and boyhood and a thousand precious memories of home were wafted toward me out of the valley, my sense of arrogant triumph at homecoming slowly melted away . . . yielded to a feeling of grateful astonishment. Homesickness, which in the course of the years had ceased to trouble me, assailed me powerfully in this last quarter-hour. Every clump of broom near the station platform and every familiar garden fence became strangely precious to me, and I asked each to forgive me for having been able to forget it and get along without it for so long."
Herman Hesse in *Youth, Beautiful Youth.*

(From *Schon Ist Die Jugend*, S. Fischer Verlag, as taken from an English translation appearing in *German Stories and Tales,* edited by Robert Pick, published by Pocket Books, Inc., 630 Fifth Ave., New York, N. Y.)

In these last few pages I wish I could account for that "strange preciousness" which most residents of Camp Dennison admit binds them to their homes. The reader might be thinking that we have found ourselves here by virtue of occupation or the simple task of finding a place to live. But while preparing this book, I found a great many people who are really in love with the town, and who will not seek to live anywhere else. They have said simply, "We like it here." And not a few have returned to Camp Dennison after many years of travel, commenting upon what an idyllic spot this is. The quotation at the beginning of this chapter dedicates it to those whose faithfulness and honesty tell them their hearts are still bound to their birthplace.

CAMP DENNISON TODAY

The population of approximately 600 is almost entirely housed in single units. The closest hospital is nine miles away, in Mariemont, although there are several doctors in the neighboring town of Milford.

Our children travel by bus to the consolidated school of Indian Hill for kindergarten and all twelve grades, or to St. Andrew's Parochial School in Milford for the first six grades.

Our businesses include the tavern, automobile service station, grocery (and post office), gravel pit, concrete block and brickcrete plant.

For Protestants there are the Methodist and Negro Baptist churches; for the Roman Catholics, St. Andrew's in Milford.

The Hamilton County and Cincinnati Bookmobile still arrives the fourth Thursday of the month.

All roads are paved, but the State Route 126 is rather rough until you reach U. S. 50 in Milford. We have all utilities, but no sewerage system, and this each builder must solve for himself within county health law limits.

Entertainment outside the home is provided by first class restaurants, a drive-in theatre, and one cinema in nearby Milford. There one also finds excellent markets, dry goods and clothing stores, as well as hardware, drugs, lumbers, and services usually found in a town of fair size.

At the moment no social, youth, or charitable groups apart from the churches are functioning in Camp Dennison. Neither do we have bus service through the village. The bus line from Cincinnati stops in Milford.

In Ohio the smallest administrative unit, except the school district, is the township. We live in Symmes township, which was created from Sycamore Township in 1825. There are twelve such townships in Hamilton County, and if a township is regularly formed it is usually six miles square. Every two years, two trustees, or a trustee and a clerk, are elected. This method insures that only two men at a time enter the office, thus making the transmission of duties easier. The clerk has no voting power, but acts as recorder, secretary, and treasurer. Meetings are held at the township seat, Symmes (which is across the Miami River from Branch Hill on Blain Street), the first Saturday of every month. These meetings are conducted in the Township Hall, and are open to the public.

The duties of the three trustees are maintaining roads not supervised by county or state, and caring for cemeteries. The roads in Camp Dennison under township care are: (Running north and south) Kilgore, Munson, Center and Daniels; (east and west) Heaton, Zumstein, Ulrich, Campbell, Jackson, Lincoln (from Daniels to Camp Road), Washington, Adams Lane and Pinkvoss Lane (which has a right of way to Camp Road). All of these with the exception of Zumstein and Munson are asphalt coated. Road work is paid for by a method known as "force account," that is, per gallon of material and per man hour, rather than contracting in advance for a certain fee. County equipment is employed if available, otherwise work is done by private businesses.

All matters pertaining to cemeteries must be conducted or approved by the township trustees.

Property line disputes may be settled by the trustees, who then assess the owners for costs, for the percentages they receive from liquor license revenue, gasoline and real estate taxes must be used exclusively for the maintenance of roads, bridges and cemeteries.

The Constable and Justices of the Peace do not receive regular salaries from the township.

Activities of the Symmes Township trustees are limited to unincorporated areas such as Camp Dennison, Remington, Rural West Loveland, Sixteen-Mile-Stand and Cactus Corner, as the incorporated villages of Indian Hill and Loveland care for their own property.

Township records, kept by the clerk, extend as far back as 1901, but the earlier books are not entirely complete.

The place of voting for all elections is the Community House on Jackson Street.

The Waldsmith House Museum is open on Sunday afternoons during the Summer months. We salute this venerable house as we pass by, for finally our interest is turned toward the future. A farm of about one hundred acres has been sold to industrial interests who at this moment are surveying for building projects reportedly to be worth some three and a half million dollars. It was inevitable that the level ground, "Zone B, light industrial," which follows the railroad on the west side, would be developed. At last it seems to be about to bring the next great change in the history of Camp Dennison.

BUILDINGS AND RESIDENCES

1. Freeman
2. Sloan
3. Rahn
4. Waldsmith Home
5. Pinkvoss
6. Little
7. Roflow
8. Robinson
9. Wells
10. Dority
11. Brumagen
12. Littlejohn
13. G. White
14. Singleton
15. Hathman
16. Krome Grocery
17. J. Miller
18. Leiman
19. Rabe
20. Dale
21. Edwards
22. Lanningham
23. Campbell
24. R. Malott
25. Westerbeck
26. Hardin
27. Labitzke
28. Bozdog
29. Stallard
30. McManus
31. Gonyer
32. Shockman
33. Crescent Nook DAV
34. Brewster
35. Tony
36. Westerkamm
37. Cain
38. Weaver
39. Carroll
40. Rose
41. Schultz
42. Buecker
43. Malott (G.)
44. Burroughs
45. Miles
46. Smith
47. Lockwood
48. Allen
49. Sparks
50. Reichert
51. Frazier
52. H. Hughes

53. Broadus
54. Brock
55. Pollit
56. Davis
57. McQuiddy
58. Pottinger
59. Warner
60. Littlejohn
61. Cisco
62. Elston
63. Tavern
63A. Apartments
64. H. Cannon
65. Littlejohn
66. Smith-Drusell
67. T. Caldwell
68. Showers
69. White (J.)
70. Myers
71. Eberhart
72. Fletcher
73. Empty
74. Galvin
75. Quayle
76. Robinson
77.
78. Hillard
79. Block Plant and Brickcrete Co.
80. Schoolhouse
81. Gant
82. Faul
83. Oligee
84. J. Martin
85. Weaver
86. McClain
87. Williams
88. W. Brown
89. Prather
90. Baptist Church
91. Jones
92. W. Caldwell
93. Anderson
94. H. Caldwell

95. J. Ferguson
96. Sims
97. H. Robinson
98. Service Station
99. Walton-Henderson
100. Richards
101. Monjar
102. Hunter
103. Rahn
104. James Martin
105. Knicely-Reeder
106. Pitser
107. Meyers
108. F. Drusell
109. I. Miller
110. Moses
111. Quinn
112. Curless
113. Falch
114. Howell, G.
115. Howell, E.
116. Pennington
117. Marsh
118. Hazard
119. Rudder
120. Felix
121. Strickland
122. McDaniel
123. Methodist Church
124. Community House
125. Turner-Holden
126. H. Brown
127. Ganz
128. Reynolds
129. Stribling
130. Clem
131. Eggers
132. W. Casey
133. Wuest
134. Elston
135. Krome

136. Dunn-Purty
137. Maphet
138. C. Ferguson
139. Combs
140. Montag
141. Yeager
142. Swaim
143. Hatcher
144. Lacinek
145. Dangler
146. D. Carter
147. H. Carter
148. Cochran (empty)
149. Adams
150. Smith
151. Empty
152. Greene
153. Wartnaby
154. Fry
155. Siebler
156. Taylor
157. Walls
158. McKnight
159. Schoettker
160. Vogt
161.
162. Schmidt
163. F. Tingley
164. Judd
165. Leever
166. Allen
167. E. Tingley
168. J. Miller
169. Hixson
170. Russell
171. Carter
172. Wethington
173. Forbeck
174. Philpot
175. Schwartz
176. Eltzroth
177. Falgner

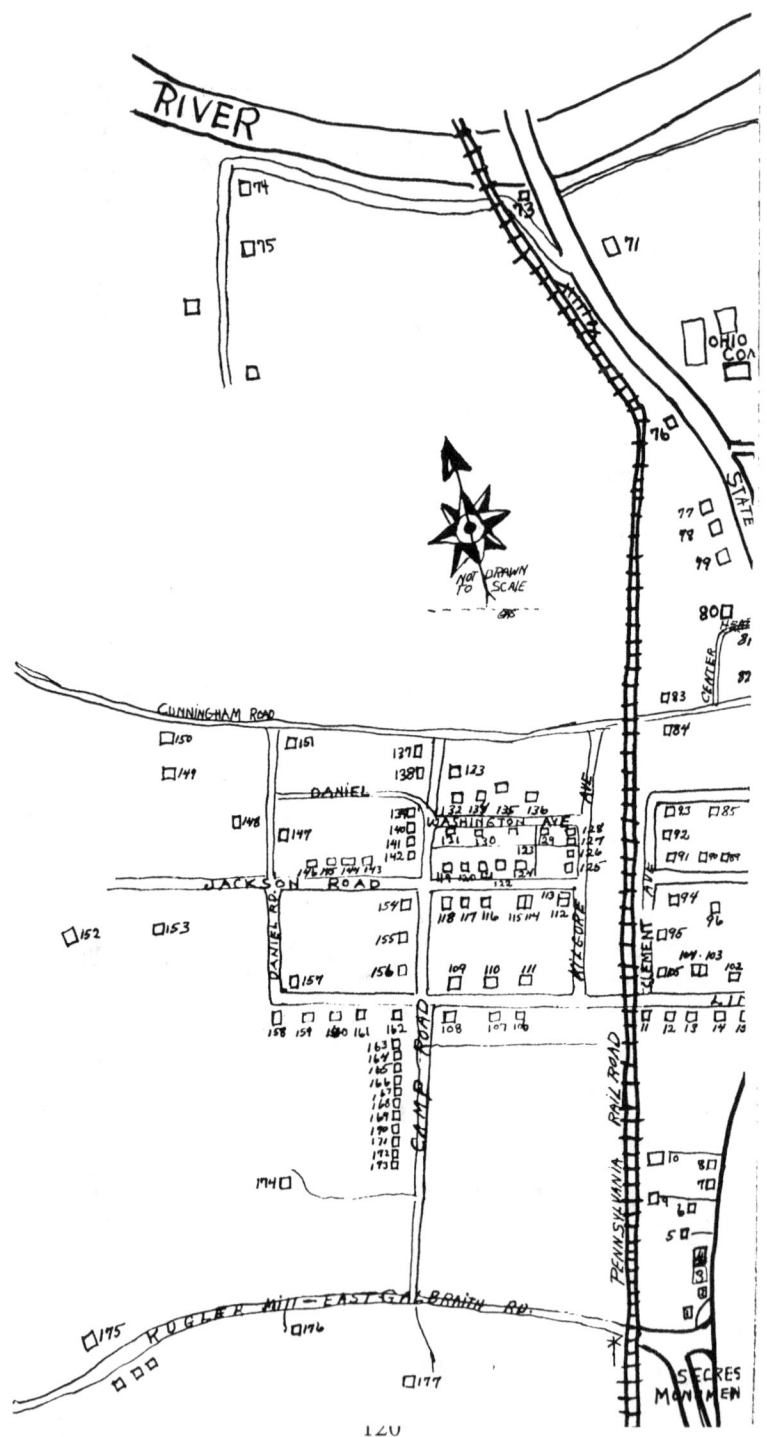

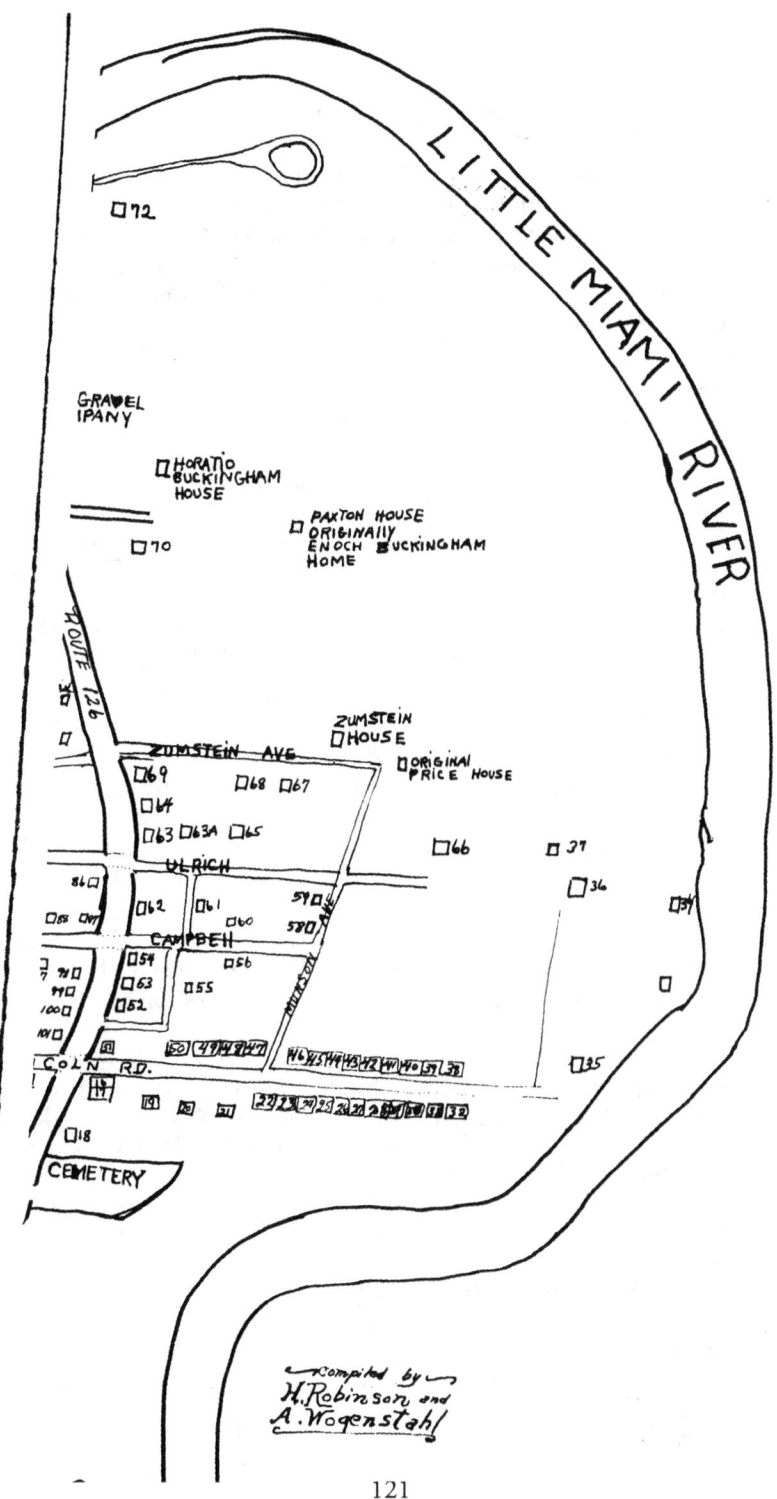

BIBLIOGRAPHY

Abraham Lincoln by Lo:.' Chesterfield, Garden City Publishing Co., Garden City, New York, 1917.

Annual Conference Minutes of the Cincinnati Conference, 1806 to 1955; Historical Library, Ohio Wesleyan University, Delaware, Ohio; and District Office of Methodist Church, Plum St., Cincinnati, Ohio.

Bulletin, Historical and Philosophical Society of Ohio, Vol. 5, No. 1, March 1947; Vol. 10, No. 3, July 1952.

The Elliott Families (1762-1911), compiled by Simon Elliott, Princeton, Illinois, 1911.

History of Cincinnati and Hamilton County, S. B. Nelson & Co., Publishers, Cincinnati, Ohio, 1894.

History of Clermont County, Ohio, 1795-1880; compiled by J. L. Rockey, R. J. Bancroft and others, publ. by Louis H. Everts, Philadelphia, Penna., 1880.

History of Ohio Methodism, by J. M. Baker, Ph.D., Curts & Jennings, Cincinnati; Eaton & Mains, New York; 1898.

History of Pleasant Plain, Ohio, by Nelson Stewart; publ. by Benj. F. Klein, Cincinnati, Ohio, 1952.

Liberty Hall, Cincinnati, Ohio, Dec. 1, 1811.

The Little Miami Railroad, Robert L. Black, Cincinnati, Ohio, (1941).

Madisonville Methodist Church manuscript, dated 1870, obtained through Mildred Bowen, Madisonville, Cincinnati, Ohio.

Memoirs of the Miami Valley, Ed. by W. C. Culkins, publ. by Robert O. Law Co., Chicago, Ill., 1919. Vols. I, II, III.

Newspaper Clippings on Cincinnati, Vol. II, Cincinnati Public Library.

The Ohio Township Officers Guide, containing all sections of the Ohio General Code applicable to township affairs including Ohio Road and School Laws, by Wm. M. Rockel, revised by George C. Trautwein, W. H. Anderson Co., Cincinnati, Ohio. Revised periodically.

Ohio Township Officers Manual with forms annotated by Charles P. Baker, Jr., Banks-Baldwin Co., Cleveland, Ohio. Revised periodically.

Pictures of Early Methodism in Ohio, by Samuel W. Williams; Jennings & Graham, Cincinnati; Eaton & Mains, New York; 1909.

They Sang As They Walked, booklet published by Milford Methodist Church, 1938.

APPENDIX

INSCRIPTIONS ON HEADSTONES IN
THE WALDSMITH CEMETERY, CAMP DENNISON,
HAMILTON COUNTY, OHIO

Bulletin of the Historical and Philosophical Society of Ohio, Volume 10, Number 3, July 1952. (published here with permission of the editors)

Anderson	David, 1881-1948
Anderson	Dora, 1888-
Bodley	Meta Telgmann, 1888-1926
Boone	Elizabeth, wife of Joseph Boone; d. Aug. 24, 1854; aet. 62 yr., 4 m., 4 d.
Boone	Harriet, dau. of Joseph and Elizabeth Boone; d. June 7, 1845; aet. 16 yr.
Boone	Joseph, son of Joseph Boone; d. Nov. 21, 1844; aet. 23 yr., 7 m.
Boone	Permelia, dau. Jos. & E. Boone, d. Jan. 5 (date buried under ground)
Boone	William, son of Joseph Boone; d. Nov. 7, 1839; aet. 21 yr. (The name may have been Bohne from Pennsylvania)
Brown	Conrad, 1826-1898
Brown	Rosina, wife of Conrad Brown; b. Mar. 2, 1832; d. June 12, 1888.
Brown	Theresa, wife of Conrad Brown; 1842-1917
Burchill	Ella, 1863-1948
Burchill	Thomas, 1858-1916
Burdsal	see Roedecker
Coldovey	see Cotton
Cotton	Margaret Coldovey, dau. of David and Elizabeth Cotton; d. May 16, 1857; aet. 16 yr., 9 m., 12 d.
Crawford	Eliza J., wife of Sisco Crawford; 1856-1926
Crawford	Sisco, 1847-1935
Daily	Alice Walton, wife of Philip Daily; 1868-1930
Daily	Philip, see Alice Daily
Danger	Herman, 1860-1927
Danger	see Meta Pinkvoss
Davis	Eliza, 1878-19—
Davis	Charles B., 19—
Davis	William, 1871-1940

Dobyns	Lou E., dau. of J. W. & B. D. Dobyns; b. June 17, 1884; d. May 2, 1896
Dobyns	Wesley; Co. C., 109 U.S.O.I.
Fox	Estella, 1888-1888
Fox	Stanley, 1889-1896
Given	Cornelia Ann., dau. of J. & S. Given; d. Sept. 16, 1847
Groff	see Reva Wiggins
Haffenbradl	Joseph, 1858-1924
Haffenbradl	Sophia, 1867-1917
Haller	Heinrich, b. Feb. 1, 1869, d. Sept. 29, 1886
Heaton	Daniel, b. Feb. 18, 1814; d. Apr. 27, 1873
Kindt	Elmer, 1901-1944
Kugler	Catherine Elizabeth, wife of Matthias Kugler; (eldest dau. of Christian Waldsmith), d. Apr. 26, 1846; aet. 65 yr., 8 mo., 17 d.
Kugler	Christian, 3rd son of Matthias Kugler; d. Apr. 19, 1836; aet. 21 yr.
Kugler	Jacob, d. Aug. 27, 1856; aet. 31 yr., 3 m. 29 d.
Kugler	Matthias, d. March 7, 1854; aet. 74 yr., 25 d.
Leever	J. W., 1832-1915
Leever	Martha J., wife of J. W., 1826-1914
Lefeber	Charles A., son of J. & S. Lefeber; d. July 16, 1849; aet. 13 d.
Lefeber	Francis P., son of J. & S. Lefeber; d. June 9, 1851; aet. 4 m., 27 d.
Lefeber	James, see Sarah
Lefeber	Sarah, wife of James Lefeber; d. July 11, 1849; aet. 37 yr., 19 d. (This name is also spelled Lafeber and Lefevre)
Letcher	Edward, 1864-1928 "Father"
Letcher	Susan D., 1864-1930 "Mother"
Long	James, d. July 11, 1849; aet. 19 yr., 4 m., 16 d.
McDowell	May Inez, dau. of J. & J. McDowell; b. Aug. 28, 1862; d. Jan. 20, 1863
McLean	Agnes P., 1847-1886
Madden	Amanda T., b. Feb. 27, 1825; d. Feb. 21, 1829
Maygors	Ella Jane, dau. of Wm. B. and Harriet Maygors (no dates given)
Moore	Arletha, 1898-1944
Moore	Frank, 1891-1944; "Wagoner, 813, O. Pioneer Inf."
Ogg	John M., d. Jan. 26, 1848; aet. 4 yr., 2 mo., 6 d.

Orr	Ambrose, son of A. & E. Orr; d. Dec. 8, 1847; aet. 17 yr., 8 mo., 16 d.
Orr	Ambrose, d. Dec. 3, 1829; aet. 15 yr., 11 m., 14 d.
Orr	Andrew, b. July 18, 1775; d. Apr. 24, 1839 (This name might have been Andreas Orth from Pennsylvania)
Pinkvoss	Dorothea S., b. Aug. 20, 1820; d. Feb. 23, 1909
Pinkvoss	Edna S., 1882-1940
Pinkvoss	Elsa, b. Apr. 30, 1884; d. Nov. 12, 1894
Pinkvoss	Henry F., b. April 29, 1882 [1839]; d. Aug. 18, 1921
Pinkvoss	Henry M., 1881-19—
Pinkvoss	Meta Dangers, wife of H. F. Pinkvoss; mother of Rolf, Henry, Elsa, b. May 18, 1853; d. Dec. 8, 1890
Poe	Cora, wife of C. P. Poe; 1871-1895
Post	Eliza, d. May 2, 1887; aet. 78 yr.
Pray	Stephen, son of J. W. and S. Pray; d. June 30, 1839; aet. 9 mo., 15 d.
Price	Abner N., 1860-1944
Price	Albert P., son of N. & E. Price; d. Oct. 10, 1868; aet. 24 yr., 2 m., 3 d.
Price	Amanda, wife of William Pray; 1840-1923
Price	Catherine, wife of Daniel Price; d. Nov. 8, 1818; aet. 55 yr., 1 m., 27 d.
Price	Daniel, d. Apr. 8, 1825; aet. 65 yr., 4 mo., 13 d.
Price	Elizabeth, wife of Nimrod Price; d. Sept. 13, 1821; aet. 22 yr., 9 mo., 3 d.
Price	Ella A., 1861-1931
Price	Jeremiah, d. Aug. 17, 1870; aet. 80 yr., 9 d.
Price	John D., son of Nimrod and Elizabeth Price; d. Feb. 28, 1826; aet. 8 yr., 9 mo., 11 d.
Price	Nimrod, d. Oct. 26, 1874; aet. 81 yr., 2 m., 12 d.
Price	Walter, d. Aug. 25, 1942; aet. 82 yr., 11 m., 3 d.
Price	William P., 1847-1932 (The name Price might have been Daniel Preisch from Penna.)
Quinn	Marilyn, dau. of Charlie and Marie Quinn; 1928-1929
Roedecker	Jacob H., 1827-1849
Roedecker	John B., 1833-1849
Roedecker	Mary, wife of William Roedecker; 1790-1868
Roedecker	Mary R., wife of J. W. Burdsal; 1829-1849
Roedecker	William, 1802-1837

Sherman	Malinda Ann, 1842-1905
Snodgrass	George K., Co. O.
Sternmann	Henry, "born in Montgomery Co., Penn.," June 14, 1778; d. June 5, 1859 (Believe this is Stroman)
Telgmann	Elsa, "Mother" (no dates)
Telgmann	Carl, "Father" (no dates)
Telgmann	Meta, see Bodley
Terrell	Octavia, wife of William Terrell; 1848-1915
Terrell	William, 1841-1921
Vandever	Henry, 1853-1859
Vandever	Lavelia A., 1848-1859
Waldsmith	Christian, d. March 30, 1814; aet. 59 yr., 7 d. (A bronze tablet states below his name "Revolutionary Soldier, 1775-1783")
Waldsmith	William (son of Christian Waldsmith). d. Nov. 7, 1816; aet. 21 yr., 9 m.
Walton	Alice, see Daily
Walton	Fannie, 1866-1933 — "Mother"
Walton	Louis S., 1864-1945 — "Father"
Wiggins	Christian V., b. Nov. 12, 1811; d. Aug. 4, 1830
Wiggins	Reva Groff, d. 1895
Wiggins	Sarah, b. Feb. 12, 1789; d. Oct. 6, 1844
Wiggins	Thomas, b. Dec. 9, 1785; d. Sept. 27, 1823
Wiggins	Thomas B., 1822-1878 (This name could be that of Valentine Weigans of Penna.)
Worsham	Charlie, 1851-1915
Worsham	Clara W., 1876-1907
Worsham	Clarence D., 1883-19—
Worsham	Isabelle E., 1890-19—
Worsham	Maude G., 1885-1896
Worsham	Sylvira, 1857-1931

There are many more burials with merely a large rock from the river used as a headstone. There is such a place beside the grave of Christian Waldsmith, presumably that of his first wife, Catherine Elizabeth Bollender.

COPY OF DEED IN THE HAMILTON'S COUNTY
RECORDER'S OFFICE

Know all men by these presents, that I, C. Waldsmith of Hamilton County, Sycamore Township and the State of Ohio, have granted and confirmed to my daughter Barbara, married to William Landon, and her children and thereon forever, or else to her nearest blood kindred, a certain tract of one hundred and sixty acres of land, a part of number thirty one fifth Township and first entire Range of the Miami purchase, where said Landon now lives on, the South East Corner, at the rate of six hundred and forty dollars, without interest, to have and to hold the same as a part of a portion of my Estate. As I may think proper to divide the same as among my family hereafter or in case of death, shall be done by my executors or administrators properly authorized to make a good and lawful title as above prescribed, for which I have set to the above my hand and fixed my seal the thirteenth of August in Year of our Lord One thousand eight hundred and nine.
Attested)
Daniel Prisch) C. Waldsmith Seal
Enoch Buckingham)
   I Griffin Yeatman — Recorder of the County of Hamilton, State of Ohio,
duly authorized and commissioned, do hereby certify and attest unto all whom it may concern, that the above Instrument of writing signed by C. Waldsmith is a true copy taken from the Records in said office Viz. Book F, Sundries - Page 159. In witness whereof I have hereunto subscribed my name at Cincinnati this 14th day of January 1822.

                Griffin Yeatman
                Recorder of H. County Ohio

CHRISTIAN WALDSMITH FAMILY

Christian Waldsmith son of Rev. John Waldsmith (born 1724 in Nassau, Germany, d. 1786 Lancaster County, Penna.) and Maria Elisabetha Grub (d. 1803) Waldschmidt who were married in 1754.

Christian Waldsmith (1755-1814) m. Catherine Bollender (d. 1810) in 1780, Reading Town, Penna.

   I. Catherine Elizabeth (1781-1846) m. Matthias Kugler (1780-1854) in 1798.
      A. John m. (1) Matilda Brower
                No children
          (2) Rebecca West
                No children

B. Matthias m. Matilda Conley
   1. Julia
   2. Josephine
   3. Harry
   4. John

C. David m. Malinda Marlay (daughter of a minister)
   1. Mathias m. Louise Miller
      (Mathais attended dedication of Secrest Monument)
      a. Marlay
      b. Howard
   2. Elizabeth Catherine m. Oliver L. Perin
      a. William Marley m. Alice Eakle
         (1) Oliver William m. Amy Bosworth Aiken
            Cynthia
            John Marlay
         (2) Marjorie Alice m. Marshall C. Hunt
            Marshall Jr.
            Sandra Perin
            Holly Ann
      b. Anna Florence m. William H. Brickel
         (1) Imogene Perin Brickel m. Charles Willig
            Barbara
            Caroline
         (2) Gladys m. Lawrence Menninger
            No children
         (3) Frances m. Arthur Dondero
            No children
         (4) Elizabeth m. Ernest Seeman
            No children
         (5) William H. m. Ruth _____
      c. Oliver M. Perin, Jr. m. Jessie Stewart.
      Nine children - live in Florida
      d. Martha Cline m. Harry T. Wernke
      Children died in infancy
      e. Ella Perin m. James K. Dean
      Nine children - live in Tennessee and Florida
      f. Mary Jane m. Clifford Todd
         (1) Clifford Jr. m. (1) Katherine Cost
            Thomas Walter Todd m. Audre Worz
            Joanne
              m. (2) Hilda Freudenthaler
            John Harry
         (2) Ethel Perin Todd m. Harold A. Manderson
            Martha Perin
            Sally

       (3) Hawley m. Barabara Herrick
           David Herrick Todd
           Ruth Perin
           Clifford
           Hawley, Jr.
       (4) Frank Perin m. Natalie Broeman
           Frank Perin Todd, Jr.
           Mark Edward
           Robert Broeman
           Theresa Ann
           Mary Sue
           Karen Joanne
  g. Bessie died in infancy
  h. Ruth Perin m. William W. Crothers
     Children died in infancy
  i. Ethel m. Samuel M. Glaughlin
  j. Harvey died in infancy
3. Marley
4. Annie m. Dr. John Price
  a. Lillyann
  b. John
5. William (a minister) m. Bertha Cory
  a. Lois
  b. Amy
  c. Hester
  d. William Alexander m. Louise Austin
     3 sons
     1 daughter
6. Charles died young
7. Christine m. Daniel Runyan
  a. Frank m. _____
     (1) Harriet
  b. Ralph died young
  c. Herbert m. Ruth Van Pelt
     (1) Richard Van Pelt Runyan m. Marj'ie Sisson
         Melinda Marlay)
         Marjorie Hamilton) twins
         Anne
     (2) Donald m. _____
         3 children
8. Virginia m. _____ Gilbert
9. Joseph Climer (Dr.) m. Ella Cummins
  a. Margaret
10. Frank Elbert (Dr.) m. Julie Closterman
  a. Frank Elbert, Jr. (Dr.)

D. Jacob
E. Christian (1804-1836)
F. Christian (1817-   )

G. Sarah (1808-   ) m. Eugene Ogg
   1. Christian
H. Christine (1812-   ) m. Edward Johnson Turpin
   1. Rebecca
   2. Mary m. _____ Gerard
   3. Denia m. _____ Wilson
   4. Flora m. _____ McCurdy
   5. Kate
   6. Alice m. William Turner Ragland
      a. Lawrence
      b. Clarence m. Pearl Judd
         (1) Lawrence m. Margaret Keeler
            Gerald
         (2) Clarence Sargent m. Mildred Kemp
            Donald Robert
            Sally Deane
   7. Edward J., Jr., m. Pauline _____
      a. Bertha m. _____ Sloan
         (1) Samuel
         (2) Edward Turpin
      b. Christine m. _____ Fischer
         (1) Mary Charlotte m. _____ Young
            Douglass
            Mary Catherine
      c. Cornelia m. _____ Cavett
         (1) Donald
         (2) Martha Lenherr
         (3) Carolyn N. Gordon
   8. Robert Worth m. (1) Eva Hutchinson
              (2) _____ Paxton
              No children
I. Ethel m. _____ McDonald
J. Catherine m. Dr. Josiah Drake
   1. Matthias
   2. Dr. Josiah T. (1846-   ) m. Fanny Curtis Simms
   3. Ada Paulina
   4. Emma Amelia m. _____ Gibbs
   5. Elizabeth Love m. Dr. Philip B. Gatch in 1855
      a. Katie D. (d. 1872)
      b. Lillian Love
      c. Florence L.
      d. Clifford D.
      e. Dawson
      f. Philip B. (d. 1873)
K. Elizabeth m. George W. Shultz
   1. Emma
   2. Elizabeth

  3. Julia
  4. George
 L. Katherine (1799-1799)
 M. Jacob m. Mary C. Fisher in 1818
II. Peter (1783-1844) m. Hannah Long
 A. Jane (1807-) m. Abner Young
  1. Christian
  2. Moses
  3. William
  4. John
  5. Kay
  6. George
  7. Sarah m. James Bovard
   a. Oliver
   b. Marion
   c. Freeman Daily
   d. Melville
   e. Abner
   f. George
   g. Finley
   h. Charles Lincoln
   i. Morton Ellsworth
   j. William Sherman
   k. Ulysses Grant
   l. Maria Jane m. Lloyd Griffiths
  8. Catherine
  9. Margaret
  10. Etheline
  11. Deborah
 B. Mary (Polly) m. _____ Buckingham
 C. Julia Ann (1819-1892) m. Samuel Roseberry (1817-91)
  1. Charles Wesley
  2. Harriet Florence
  3. Electra Jane
  4. Margaret
  5. Thomas Shipp
  6. Alice
  7. Samuel Morrison
  8. Irene
  9. Luella
  10. William McKee
  11. May D.
 D. Margaret (1824-1857) m. William H. Roseberry (1820-1881) in 1841
  1. Eliza Laird m. Isham Inlow (1842-1894)
  2. Peter Waldschmidt m. Lana Hamilton (1845-1910)
  3. Jasper m. Mary Elizabeth Low (1847-1930)
  4. Mary Catherine m. Cyrus DeVilbiss (1848-1907)

       5. Samuel Austin (1851-1875)
       6. Mina Jane m. Andrew Jackson Spears (1855-1881)
       7. Margaret Julia m. Charles B. W. Bennett (1857-   )
   E. Catherine (1811-1859) m. Robert Foster (m. 1833)
       1. William Foster (1834-1859)
       2. Julia Ann (1835-1863) m. William Hoard
       3. Hannah Jane (1836-1881) m. Newton Phillips
         a. Joseph
         b. Addie
         c. Dean
         d. George
         e. Jim
         f. Eliza
         g. Florence
       4. John W. (1838-1864)
       5. Mary Celina (1843-1917) m. William Jacob Dickson
                                     (1833-1877) in 1865
         a. Lida m. William Shaffer
           Elizabeth m. Adolph W. Raab
           William D.
         b. Lulu m. John W. Russell
           William Jacob Dickson m. Ruth Berge Cottrel
           Malcolm (1893-1893)
           Rachel (1895-1895)
           Katherine (1905-   ) m. George Rainwater
         (m. 1940)
       6. Nelson L. (1845-1859)
       7. Matilda (1847-1876) m. Charles Woodard
       8. Robert L. (1848-1864) (killed in Civil War)
       9. Eliza Lydia (1850-1943) m. Samuel Caplinger
      10. Allan Waldsmith (1854-1920) m. Margaret Green
      11. Perry (1858-1858)
   F. Eliza m. Horatio N. Lard
   G. Elizabeth
   H. Peter
III. Anna Marie (1786-1786)
IV. John (1788-1814) m. Margaret Elliot (m. 4/28/1808)
   A. Jane (1809-   )
   B. John K. (1810-   )
   C. Matilda (1813-   )
 V. Christian (1793-1801)
 VI. William (1795-1816) m. Elizabeth Tice, 1812. No issue.
 VII. David (1801-1808)
VIII. Catherine (1806-   ) m. Daniel H. Horne (1788-1870.)
   A. Charles W.
Christian Waldsmith m. (2nd) Magdalena (Polly) Kern
   (widow) Custard

IX. Sarah (1812-1852) m. James Given (1808-   ), 1831
    A. Catherine Elizabeth (1835-1914) m. Lain Ready Custard
    B. Orlando (1837-1864) - 39th Regt. O.V.I.
    C. Sarah Augusta m. John Teal
        1. Orlando S. m. Myrtle Davis
           a. Alice m. Philip Deerwester
              Philip A. Frances Davison
                 Robert Philip
                 Sandra Lee
                 Gail Loraine
                 Joe Frances
              Alma m. Culver Linn
                 Susan Carol
                 Marcia Diane
                 Jeffrey
                 James T.
           b. Allen m. Irma Oberwitte
              Virginia m. James Perin
                 Dennis
                 David
                 Patricia
                 Barbara
                 Holly Ann
              Mary Jean m. Fred Meyer
                 Linda
                 Rebecca
    D. William (1842-1901) m. Josie Stewart
    E. Cornelia Ann (1844-1847)
    F. Mary Louise (1847-1916) m. Charles M. Hunt in 1868
    G. Christian Waldsmith (1849-1910) m. Lavina Stewart in 1881
    H. Cora Bell (1852-   ) m. Richard Tucker in 1872

Information obtained from Mrs. Frank Elbert Kugler, Sr., Mrs. Herbert Runyan, Mrs. Clarence Ragland, Mrs. Christine Turpin Fischer, Mrs. Alice Deerwester, Mrs. George Rainwater, History of Clermont County, and *History of Cincinnati and Hamilton County, Ohio.*

THE PECKENPAUGH FAMILY

Frederick and Elizabeth Peckenpaugh
    I. Elizabeth (b. 1792, Fayette County, Pa.) m. Joseph Boone in 1811
        A. Sarah (1812-1848) m. James LeFeber in 1835
        B. Rachel (1813-1896) m. Hezekiah Price in 1851
            1. Elizabeth Lunbeck
                a. Nellie
                b. Lela

C. William (1815-1839) buried in Camp Dennison
D. Eliza (1817-1818)
E. Susan (1819-1820)
F. Joseph (1821-1844) buried in Camp Dennison
G. Permelia (1823-1906) buried in Camp Dennison
H. Thomas (1826-1906) m. Nancy Broadwell in 1855
    1. Walter
    2. Ira
        a. Charles D.
        b. Deborah Startsman
            Daniel Boone Startsman, Jr.
    3. Deborah m. Van R. Humphrey
        a. Stella Humphrey Neal (2nd Miller)
            Two daughters
    4. Allen M.
    5. William
    6. Charles
I. Harriet (1828-1845) buried in Camp Dennison
J. Daniel Amazon
    1. Charles
    2. Elmer
    3. Eva
    4. Clara
K. Camillus (1833-1901)
    1. Ella Aiken
    2. Harry
    3. Clifford m. Elizabeth Pierce
    4. Edgar
    5. George
    6. Camillus
L. Elizabeth (1836-   ) m. Andrew Carman in 1860
    1. Mayme m. Henry Beekley
        a. One child died in infancy
        b. Benjamin, died in infancy
        c. Florence m. Marshall Weigel
            Evelyn Weigel Shomberg
            Bernice
    2. Kate m. Richard Beekley
        a. Elizabeth m. Herbert Carman
            Ashley
            Richard
        b. Carman - not married
        c. Clarence
            Doris Beekley Wood
            Virginia Beekley Jones
        d. Joseph - now deceased
    3. Austin Carman m. Irene Krehnbrink
    4. Emma

      5. Elizabeth
      6. Nellie died in infancy
      7. Amelia
II. Rachel (1808-   ) m. Nimrod Price in 1823 (See Price genealogy)
III. Catherine (Kate) (1800-1873) m. John Cunningham in 1818
   A. George (1819-1823)
   B. Frederick Peckenpaugh (1821-1852)
   C. Sarah Ducket (1823-1846) m. Granderson T. Ducket
   D. Eliza Ann Perry (1825-1854)
   E. John (1827-   )
   F. William B. (1829-1906) m. (1) Selina Pancoat in 1855
                                  m. (2) Mary R. Montford in 1867
      1. Harry
      2. Lucien
      3. Clarence
      4. Florence
      5. Ed
      6. Blanche Kendall
      7. Agnes
      8. William
      9. Elmer
   G. Albert James (1833-1912) m. Priscilla C. Losh (1841-1910) in 1861
      1. Helen C. Harris
      2. Alma Mary
      3. Alasanna C. Mayer
      4. Lillian Bell
      5. Albert James Jr.
      6. Emma Catharine Ginter
      7. Frances Edna Raschig
      8. Eldon Losh
   H. Hendrick (1834-   )
   I. Catharine Jane (1836-   )
   J. Elizabeth Hughes (1838-1887)
   K. Harriet Melissa (1840-1860)
   L. Prudence Irene (1843-   )
IV. Polly Snell (no information available)
V. Prudence Compton (no information available)
VI. Nancy m. Henry Terwilleger (both buried in Peckenpaugh Cemetery which is located on what is now the Kroger property)
   A. Frederick Peckenpaugh Terwillegar (1831-1914) m. Nancy McCullough in 1851
      (Note spelling of last name is changed)
      1. Harriet - d.i.
      2. Amanda - d.i.

3. Sarah Elizabeth (1856-1889) m. Charles Motsinger
   a. Myrtle
   b. Ernest
   c. Nancy
4. Catherine Jane m. Jos. Shumard in 1894
   a. Four children who died in infancy
5. Byron m. Elizabeth Helen _____ in 1887
   a. Clyde
6. Frederick Leander (1863-1921) m. Catherine Cornuelle
   a. Byron Clyde
      2 children (one of them Robert from whom this information was obtained)
   b. Stella Maria
   c. Paul Cornuelle
   d. Theodore Samuel
6. Alva Dorr (spelling may be wrong) - went away as a young man and never heard of again

B. Christina born in Camp Dennison in 1835, d. 1909, m. **Joe Drake**
   1. Hal
   2. Joe m. Annie McGill
      a. Ross
         1 child
   3. Al m. Jennie Orr
   4. Edward m. Alice Warbington
      a. Marie Drake
   5. Ada m. Jake Worstel
      a. Maud
      b. Hazel
   6. Eva (1873-1881)

C. Steward Terwilleger (1836-1911) born in Camp Dennison m. Jennie Johnston in 1867
   1. Miles
   2. Jennie June m. Sam Linnenkamp
   3. **William**
      a. William
      b. Jack
   4. May m. _____ Collier
   5. Earl died young

VII. Permelia m. Abraham Terwilleger
   A. John
   B. William
   C. Fred
   D. Gus
   E. Leon or Alonzo

Note: The parents of Henry and Abraham Terwilleger were John and Catherine Buckingham Terwilleger. All their children

were: Harvey, Abraham, Henry, John, William (b. 1811) and Lewis (b. 1812).
VIII. Frederick (1814-   ) m. Delilah Springsteel
   A. Elizabeth - died in infancy
   B. John - died in infancy
   C. Marcus - died in infancy
   D. Frederick - died in infancy
   E. Mary (1838-1856)
   F. Martha (1844-   ) m. (1) Sam Losh
      1. Charles Losh
            m. (2) ———— Purdue
   G. Charles (1852-1914) m. (1) Jennie Cosbey (d. 1887)
      1. Frederick Lee - died in infancy
            m. (2) Minnie Drake in 1898
      2. Evelyn May - died in infancy
      3. Carroll Charles m. Thelma Zimmers
      4. Frederick G. (Ted) m. Arnetta Taylor
      5. Ruth m. Bryan Brunner
         a. Robert
           One daughter
      6. Russell m. Louise Goedde

Information on the above obtained from Mrs. Deborah Startsman, Terrace Park; Mrs. Florence Weigel, Hyde Park; Frances Raschig, Hyde Park; History of Hamilton County; Anna Meyer, Mason; Robert Terwillegar, Mariemont; and Ruth Peckenpaugh Brunner, now of Philadelphia

THE PRICE FAMILY

Daniel (d. 1825) and Catharine (d. 1818) Price
  I. Nimrod m. (1) Elizabeth ———— who died in 1821 at age of 22
    A. John D. (died in 1826 at age of 8)
       (2) Rachel Peckenpaugh in 1823
    B. Marcus m. Sarah Briley
      1. Lloyd
      2. Walter
      3. Ida m. Charles Briggs
      4. Edward m. Ida Potts from Guinea, O.
      5. Enos (married and eventually disappeared)
      6. Millie m. Joe Stevens
         Two children
    C. Martha Jane m. (1) ———— Vandever
        1. Charles Vandever
            m. (2) John Leever, Guinea, O.
        2. Ed Leever

D. Amanda m. (1) _____ Hutchinson, Guinea, O.
   1. Jeff
      a. Two sons
   2. Belle
      m. (2) _____ Apgar, Guinea
         Moved to Illinois and had a large family
      m. (3) _____ Shipley
E. John
   1. Flora m. Charles Sellers
   2. James
F. Mahlon
   1. Oscar
   2. Herbert
   3. Anna m. Joe Condo
   4. Rachel m. Ed King
G. Marius (Brown)
   1. Wesley m. Roy Foster (they died in Colorado)
     Several children
   2. Lena m. _____ Foster
   3. Genevieve m. Harry Osborne
      a. Hal Osborne, teacher in Chicago - retired
   4. Lillian m. Walter Osborne
      a. Jesse Price Osborne (lawyer)
   5. Albert (d. 1944) and wife Ella (d. 1931) buried
     in Camp Dennison
      a. Josephine
      b. Brown who lives in Tennessee
H. Enos Jeremiah m. _____ Fitzwater, Guinea, O.
   1. One son
I. Milton Daniel
   1. Charles (by 1st marriage)
   2. Stella (by 2nd marriage) m. Tom Gallagher
   3. Harry
   4. George
J. Albert (died in early 20's - never married)
K. William P. m. Amanda Roberts
   1. Cora m. Claude Poe
      a. Mary Poe Heath
         Five children
            16 grandchildren
   2. William Roberts (died in 1946 - no children)
   3. Jessie m. Samuel A. Lytle
      a. Paul A. Lytle
II. Abigail m. William Buckingham (see Buckingham genealogy)
III. Jeremiah (d. 1870) m. M. Elizabeth Wiggins
   A. Sarah C. (b. 1810)
   B. Daniel (b. 1812)

C. Catharine (b. 1814)
D. Mathilda (b. 1816)
E. Malinda (b. 1818)
F. Mary W. (b. 1821)
G. John (b. 1823)
H. Elizabeth (b. 1825)
I. Martha W. (b. 1827)
J. Nimrod W. (b. 1829 - died in infancy)
K. Mahala O. (b. 1831)
L. Rachel A. (b. 1833)
M. Jeremiah Jr. (b. 1835) m. Louise Orr Fitzwater
    1. William Perley Price m. Alma Smizer
       a. E. W. Price, Mulberry, Ohio
    2. Eleanor Price m. (1) Charles Shaw
                   (2) Orin Hill

Information on Price family obtained from Mrs. Jessie Price Lytle and Mr. E. W. Price.

BUCKINGHAM FAMILY

William Buckingham (1734-1829) m. Jane Jones (1744-1826)
    (parents of Enoch and Levi)
  I. Enoch Buckingham (1763-1845) m. Mary Jeffries (1771-1829)
    (The first Enoch and Levi, twin sons of Enoch, died in infancy)
    A. Levi (1796-   ) m. Eliza Bell (daughter of Peter and Margaret Bell)
       1 William
       2. Eliza
       3. Harriet
       4. Margaret
       5. John
       6. Robert
    B. William (1791-1878) m. Abigail Price (1789-1841)
       1. William (1809-1899) m. Amy _____ (lived in Illinois)
          a. Abbie
          b. John or Jehu
          c. Marcus
          d. Alfred
          e. Enoch
          f. Ambrose m. Josephine, daughter of John S. Buckingham
          g. Harriet m. Elliot Humphrey
       2. Benjamin (1811-1851) m. Margaret Elliot
          a. Maria
          b. William

     c. Harriet
     d. Martha Ann
3. Nimrod (1812-   )
4. Mary (1814-1881)
5. Catherine (1816-1881)
6. Ambrose (1818-1830)
7. Euphemia (1820-1823)
8. Harriet A. (1822-1862) m. Rev. James Maple
9. Andrew Jackson (1824-1902) m. Louisa Ramsey
     a. Isabella
     b. Sarah L. (Lou) m. William Hamilton
         (1) Robert, died at 23 years of age
         (2) William, died at 18 years of age
     c. Alwilda m. Benjamin Meyers
         Daughter died in infancy
     d. Kate m. Rev. James Maple
     e. Maud m. John Henry Meyer
10. Ann (1826-1890) m. John Ramsey
     a. William
     b. Adelia
     c. Arselia
     d. Frances
     e. Etta
11. Oliver Perry (1830-1887) m. Eliza Jane Weller
     a. Harry Montford m. Luella Humphrey
         (1) Mack
         (2) Ray m. Opal Dillon
             Richard
             Ray m. Rita Eschmeyer
                 Elaine Ann
                 Pamela Jean
                 Patricia Rae
         (3) Stanley m. Kathryn Plum
             Patricia
             Ray
         (4) Brookfield m. Letty Smith
             Roger
             Malcolm
             Artis
         (5) Juliet m. Ray Jones
             Robert A. m. Jane Crumrine
                 Richard Bruce
                 Sandra Jean
         (6) Alfred m. Doris Rogers
             Oliver
             Harry
             Anne
             William

    b. Lee m. Fannie Swan
      (1) Genevieve m. Frank Arnold
          Mary Miles m. Anthony Given
          Sarah Lee
      (2) Lee Swan
          Jean
          Elizabeth
    c. Lola m. Charles Mosteller
      (1) **Forest**
      (2) **Albert**
      (3) **Laura**
      (4) **Louella**
      (5) **Edna**
    d. Florence m. William Bonnell
      (1) Lola
      (2) Harold m. Mary Dettmer
          Mary Lee
          Jean
  12. Alfred (Dr.) (1832-1912) m. Edna Van Pelt
    a. Marcia Lucia
  13. Isaiah or Isaac (1836-   )
  Also either one or two sets of twins who died in infancy
C. Jane (1791-1878) d. _____ Black
  1. A. Black
  2. Jeff
  3. Margaret
  4. Lee
  5. Marie m. _____ Dewey
D. Enoch A. (1788-1853) m. Belinda Robinson
  1. Mary Ann m. John Thompson
    a. Robinson
    b. Rose m. Oliver Holloway
      (1) Edna Wagner
          2 children
      (2) Mary Henshaw
          2 children
      (3) John m. Alma Hoppe
          2 children
      (4) Chester m. Mildred Freeman
          3 children
      (5) Ruth m. Richard Brower
          2 children
      (6) Frank died at 15 years
      (7) Oliver died at 2 years
    c. Franklin, D.I.
    d. Phoebe, D.I.
    e. Belle, D.I.
    f. Lillie m. Simon Little (died at 24 years)

    2. Belinda died young
    3. Robinson m. Louise Hawn
    4. Samuel m. Adeline Vandervort
    5. Frank m. Mary Jane Fitzwater
       a. Belle m. Horace Dean
          (1) Robert Dean
            2 sons
       b. Harry m. (1) Lillie Meyer
            m. (2) Grace Applegate Stewart
E. Washington
F. Greenbrier (1812-1852)
G. Mark (1809-1877) m. Margaret Hawn
    1. Mary Elizabeth
    2. Alexander D.
    3. Charlie
    4. Holly R.
    5. Ada
    6. Clifford
    7. Mark m. Myra Hutchinson
H. Horatio (1806-1877) m. (1) Jane Day
    1. Agnes m. James Paxton
       a. Horatio
       b. David
       c. Albert
    2. Charles
    3. Louise m. Minor Vandervort
       a. Jennie Day m. George H. Eveland
       b. Cortis m. Arabella Fulton
          (1) Esther
          (2) Elizabeth m. Edgar Shields
          (3) Paul m. Grace Galloway
             Janet m. John Cable
             Robert
       c. Horatio Frank m. Louise Meyer
          (1) Dorothy
          (2) Mildred
          (3) Jane m. Howard Weiner
       d. John William m. Helen Strach
Horatio m. (2) Euphemia Snyder
    4. Louis m. _____
       a. One daughter
    5. Walter m. Laura Clark
       a. Ruth m. Albert Monter
          2 sons and 2 daughters
       b. Clark m. Maud Knopp
       c. Mary m. John Monter
       d. Milton m. Helene Fischer
          (1) Milton, Jr.

6. Albert G. m. Virginia Doyle
   a. Horatio m. Susan Hutchinson
      (1) Edna Cole
      (2) Roma Flint
         Horatio
         Albert
         Lois
      (3) Eleanor
   b. Effie m. William Newbigging
      (1) Albert
   c. Alvin died young
Albert G. m. (2) Selecta Boyer
   d. Knaul m. Lillian Zacharias
      (1) Albert m. Janet Arnold
         Ann
         James Arnold
I. Maria died at early age
J. Matilda
K. John S. m. (1) Margaret Gest
   1. Josephine m. Ambrose Buckingham of Illinois
      a. Clarence
      b. John
      c. Amy
   2. William J. m. Ida Rankin
John S. m. (2) Mary Epps Ferguson
   3. John C. m. Carrie Cooper
      a. Camilla m. Wilfred Fry
         (1) Marian
         (2) Wilfred
         (3) Mary Camilla
         (4) Margaret
      b. Cooper died young
      c. Ambrose m. Hazel McCammon
      d. Clara m. Dr. George Pierrett
      e. Margaret m. Ray Conant
   4. Margaret K. m. Richard Bard Turner
      a. James B.
      b. John S.
      c. Lulu m. Edwin Thayer
         (1) Richard
         (2) Alice
         (3) Mary
         (4) John
         (5) Katherine, D.I.
      d. Viola
      e. Alice M.
      f. Mary M.

Information on the Enoch Buckingham family was obtained

from the following: Lola Bonnell, Viola Turner, Mary Turner, Mrs. Belle Dean, Mrs. Mary Monter, Mrs. Ruth Brower, Mrs. Mary Henshaw, Mrs. Edna Wagner, Mrs. George Rainwater.

II. Levi Buckingham m. Lydia Sears
   A. Smith m. Nancy Sanders
      1. Jane m. John Queal (See Queal Genealogy)
   B. Eliza m. John Fletcher
      1. Smith B. m. Lydia Patterson
         a. Claude
         b. Paul
      2. Martha m. John Moore
         a. George m. Agent Rower
      3. Maria
      4. Ann m. William Garner
         a. Wallace m. Ann Campbell
   C. Isaac A. - died at an early age
   D. Mary Jane
   E. Maria m. (1) David Buckingham
      1. Van Buren Buckingham m. Sarah Vandever
         a. Lillian m. Samuel Robinson
            (1) Julia m. Carl Volkman
                Lois
                Lee
            (2) Edward m. Winona Buckley
                Jean Ann Reeves
         b. Julia m. Lee Robinson
            (1) Harry m. Evelyn Knox
                Jerry
            (2) John m. (1) Dorothy Golden
                David
                John (Jack)
                John m. (2) Verona Johnson
         c. Alfred died when a young man
     Maria m. (2) _____ Weaver
      2. Isaac Weaver (later went by name of Buckingham)
         a. Pet
         b. Don m. Dr. Barnes
            Two sons
   F. Lydia m. William W. Fletcher (Captain in Mexican War)
      1. Levi
         a. Frank m. Ella Henninger
            (1) Stella Ertel
            (2) Wilbur
                Vonnie
            (3) Ethel Specker
                Jane Ault
                   4 children

            (4) Carl
        b. Harold
        c. Charles - died at early age
    2. Scott
    3. Phoebe m. Charles Hopkins
        a. Guy
    4. Josephine
    5. William
    6. Theresa m. George Kinney
        a. Grace m. George Sweet
            (1) Clarence
            (2) Louis m. Grace Reed
                Patrica Ann
        b. William
    7. Hall B. m. Margaret Kinney
        a. Florence m. Rolf D. Pinkvoss, D.V.M.
            (1) Henry m. Kathryn Edwards
                Richard
                Joan
        b. Julia m. Walter Cooper
            (1) William m. Ruth Haney
                Margie
                Judy
                Albert
            (2) Elizabeth died at 8 years
            (3) Florence Hutchinson
                Marcia
                Cheryl
            (4) Hall F. m. Nellie Eltzroth
                Susie
                Jon Hall
            (5) Katherine Rosenzweig
                Kathy
                David
                Jody Kay
        c. Emma m. Albert J. Doermann
        d. Clarence m. Clara Devine
            (1) William H.
                Pamela
            (2) Clarence Robert - lost life in World War II
            (3) Donald
        e. Agnes - died at early age
        f. Pierce - died in infancy
        g. Worth
III. Hannah Buckingham, sister of Enoch and Levi, married Moses Bonnell. They settled near Hamilton, Ohio.

Information on Levi Buckingham family secured from: Mrs. Florence Pinkvoss, Mrs. Julia Robinson, Mrs. Julia Volkman.

QUEAL FAMILY

Michael (1800-1877) m. Louise Mytilla Moore (1803-1901)
  I. William Henry (1827-1910) m. Mary C. (1837-1890)
    A. Minta Baker
      1. Adam
  II. Jane Connett
    A. Nell C. Detweiler
    B. Albert F. Connett
    C. Ida Martin
  III. Araminta (1825-1879) m. Otha Williams
    A. Ida Williams
    B. Millard Williams
  IV. Albert F. m. Martha B.
    A. Louisa Tudor
    B. Selina Magee
    C. Philip
    D. Anna
    E. Emily
  V. John O. (1835 1919) m. Jennie Buckingham about 1867
    A. Smith B. (1868-1943) m. Emma Cottingham in 1890
        (changed spelling to Quayle)
      1. John Matson m. Mary Motsinger
        a. Mary Jane Davis
        b. Shirley
        c. Thomas
        d. Robert
    B. William Henry (1870-   ) m. Pearl Davis
      1. John Henry
    C. George (1872-1873)
  VI. George W. m. (1) Emma _____
      A. Albert C. (died in 1892 as baby)
    George W. m. (2) Flora Mount
    B. George
  VII. Maria m. Albert B. Connett
    A. Lou
    B. Georgia
    C. Alberta
    D. Harvey

CIRCUIT RIDERS AND PREACHERS
METHODIST CHURCH, 1806-1956

Year	District	Charge or Circuit	Minister
Western Conference			
1806	Ohio	Miami	Benjamin Lakin
			Joshua Riggin
1807	Ohio	Miami	Benjamin Lakin
			John Collins
1808	Ohio	Miami	Samuel Parker
			Hector Sandford
1809	Miami	Cincinnati	William Houston
			John Sinclair
1810	Miami	Cincinnati	Solomon Langdon
			Moses Crume
1811	Miami	Cincinnati	Benjamin Lakin
			William Young
1812	Miami	Cincinnati	William Burke
			John Strange
Ohio Conference			
1813	Miami	Little Miami	Samuel Hellums
1814	Miami	Little Miami	William Burke
			Ebenezer David
1815	Miami	Cin'ti & Miami	Joseph Oglesby
			John Waterman
1816	Miami	Miami	Alexander Cummins
			Russell Bigelow
1817	Miami	Miami	Abbott Goddard
			William P. Finley
1818	Miami	Milford	David Sharp
		Miami	Benjamin Lawrence
1819	Lebanon	Miami	Samuel West
			Henry Matthews
		Milford	Samuel Brown
1820	Lebanon	Miami	William Dixon
			Robert Delap
		Milford	Burroughs Westlake
			Horace Brown
1821	Lebanon	Miami	Moses Crume
			Arthur W. Elliott
		Milford	John C. Brook
			Thomas L. Hitt
1822	Lebanon	Madison	James Jones
			James Murray
		Milford	Benjamin Lawrence
			Nathan Walker

1823	Lebanon	Madison	J. Stewart
			Nehemiah B. Griffith
		Milford	John Strange
			James T. Wells
1824	Lebanon	Madison	John F. Wright
			Thomas Hewson
		Milford	Samuel Baker
			James Smith
1825	Miami	Miami	John P. Taylor
			Augustus Eddy
		Milford	William J. Thompson
			Robert Spencer
1826	Miami	Miami	Andrew S. M'Lean
			John P. Taylor
		Milford	Arthur W. Elliott
			Robert W. Finley
1827	Miami	Miami	Andrew S. M'Lean
			Alfred M. Lorain
		Milford	Arthur W. Elliott
			Eliph J. Field
1828	Miami	Miami	W. Simmons
			D. D. Davidson
		Milford	Andrew S. McLean
			G. Gatch
1829	Miami	Miami	William Simmons
			John Stewart
1830	Miami	Miami	John Stewart
			James Laws
1831	Miami	Miami	William J. Thompson
			James Laws
1832	Miami	Miami	Adam Poe
			Chas. W. Staine
1833	Miami	Miami	Adam Poe
			B. Westlake
1834	Cincinnati	Miami	B. Westlake
			A. S. M'Lean
1835	Cincinnati	Madison	G. W. Maley
			J. G. Bruce
		Georgetown	A. S. M'Lean
			Jacob Dixon
1836	Cincinnati	Madison	Alfred M. Lorain
		Georgetown	Levi P. Miller
			Wesley Stone
1837	Cincinnati	Madison	Zachariah Connell
			Levi P. Miller
		Georgetown	Robert Cheney

1838	Cincinnati	Madison	Adam Miller
			William I. Ellsworth
1839	Cincinnati	Madison	Charles R. Lovell
			Jonathan F. Conrey
1840	Lebanon	Madison	Charles R. Lovell
			Jacob G. Dimmett
1841	Lebanon	Madison	Joseph Gasner
			Lorenzo D. Huston
1842	Lebanon	Madison	William Parrish
			Jos. A. Reeder
1843	Cincinnati	Madisonville	William Parish
1844	Cincinnati	Madisonville	Greenbury R. Jones
1845	Lebanon	Madisonville	Edward Estell
1846	Lebanon	Madisonville	Levi White
1847	East Cincinnati	Madisonville	Levi P. Miller
1848	East Cincinnati	Madisonville	Levi P. Miller
			James A. Taylor
1849	East Cincinnati	Madisonville	Joseph M. Gatch
			Joseph C. Harding
1850	East Cincinnati	Madisonville	Joseph M. Gatch
1851	East Cincinnati	Madisonville	William Langarl
			John C. Maddy

Cincinnati & Kentucky Conference

| 1852 | East Cincinnati | Madisonville | N. Westerman |
| | | | James M. Cavin |

Cincinnati Conference

1853	East Cincinnati	Madisonville	A. W. Tibbatts
			Henry Baker
1854	East Cincinnati	Madisonville	A. W. Tibbatts
			Henry Baker
1855	East Cincinnati	Madisonville	B. Glasscock
			Thomas Audas
1856	East Cincinnati	Madisonville	B. Glasscock
			A. M. Lorrain
1857	East Cincinnati	Madisonville	A. M. Lorrain
			A. Murphy
1858	East Cincinnati	Madisonville	J. F. Spence
			W. Herr, P.E.
			D. H. Sargent
1859	East Cincinnati	Madisonville	J. F. Spence
			J. C. Bontecou
1860	East Cincinnati	Madisonville	J. M. Gatch
			J. T. Bail

Year			
1861	East Cincinnati	Madisonville	J. T. Bail
			Levi White
1862	Ripley	Madisonville	E. C. Merrick
			Levi White

(Post Chaplain at Camp Dennison - N. Callendar, Member of Milford Quarterly Conference)

1863	East Cincinnati	Madisonville	S. W. Edmiston
			L. P. Miller

(Post Chaplain at Camp Dennison - N. Callendar, Member of Milford Quarterly Conference)

1864	East Cincinnati	Madisonville	S. W. Edmiston
			L. P. Miller

(Post Chaplain at Camp Dennison - N. Callendar, Member of Milford Quarterly Conference)

1865	East Cincinnati	Madisonville	David Kemper

(Post Chaplain at Camp Dennison - N. Callendar, Member of Milford Quarterly Conference)

1866	East Cincinnati	Camp Dennison & Indian Hill	N. C. Callendar
1867	East Cincinnati	Madisonville	W. Q. Shannon
			J. W. Mendenhall
1868	East Cincinnati	Madisonville	W. Q. Shannon
			Nathan Prince
1869	East Cincinnati	Newtown	William Routledge
1870	East Cincinnati	Newtown	George T. Weaver
1871	East Cincinnati	Newtown	Richard A. Arthur
1872	East Cincinnati	Newtown	Lucien M. Davis
1873	East Cincinnati	Newtown	T. J. Euens
1874	East Cincinnati	Camp Dennison	C. H. Lawton
1875-76	East Cincinnati	Camp Dennison	E. C. Smith
1877	East Cincinnati	Camp Dennison	W. J. Baker
1878	East Cincinnati	Camp Dennison	W. N. Williams
1879-80	East Cincinnati	Camp Dennison	W. E. Kugler
1881-83	East Cincinnati	Camp Dennison	C. W. Barnes
1884-85	East Cincinnati	Camp Dennison	John Wilson

(4 churches - Armstrong Chapel, Newtown, Madeira, Camp Dennison, 300 S.S. members, 250 church members)

1886	Hillsboro	Camp Dennison	John Wilson
1887	Hillsboro	Camp Dennison	A. L. Howren
1888-89	Hillsboro	Newtown	Henry Stokes
1890-92	Hillsboro	Newtown	Amos T. Cowgill
1893	Cincinnati	Newtown	Amos T. Cowgill
1894-96	Cincinnati	Newtown	Allen D. Maddox

(5 churches - Newtown, Maderia, Miamiville, Armstrong Chapel - Camp Dennison)

1897	Cincinnati	Newtown	L. M. Davis
1898-99	Cincinnati	Branch Hill	Wm. M. West

(4 churches - Branch Hill, Miamiville, Concord, Camp Dennison)

1900	Georgetown	Newtown	Lucien M. Davis
1901-02	Milford	Newtown	Lucien M. Davis
1903-05	Milford	Newtown	Thomas P. Walter

(4 churches - Newtown, Armstrong Chapel, Madeira, Camp Dennison))

1906-07	Milford	Newtown	Wm. E. Verity
1908-10	Cincinnati	Newtown	John H. Lease
1911	Cincinnati	Newtown	M. Hobson
1912-15	Cincinnati	Newtown	Christopher Stone

(Miamiville added to charge in 1914)

1916-17	Cincinnati	Newtown	O. W. Miller

(3 churches - Newtown, Camp Dennison, Miamiville)

1918	Cincinnati	Newtown	S. F. Wenger
1919	Cincinnati	Newtown	Ralph Jones
1920	Cincinnati	Newtown	No pastor
1921	Cincinnati	Camp Dennison & Miamiville	O. B. Cole

(2 churches)

1922	Cincinnati	Camp Dennison & Miamiville	Harry C. Otte

(3 churches - Camp Dennison, Miamiville, Branch Hill)

1923-45	Wilmington	Mulberry	Eugene Riffle

(5 churches - Mulberry, Concord, Perintown, Pleasant Hill, Camp Dennison)

1946	Wilmington	Camp Dennison-Miamiville	E. R. Biggs
1947	Wilmington	Camp Dennison-Miamiville	C. P. Taylor Virgil Hamilton
1948	Wilmington	Camp Dennison-Miamiville	Paul Steele
1949	Wilmington	Camp Dennison-Miamiville	John Collins
1950	Wilmington	Camp Dennison-Miamiville	F. H. Russell
1951	Wilmington	Camp Dennison-Miamiville	George R. Groh Elmer Copley
1952-56	Wilmington	Camp Dennison-Miamiville	Raymond R. Deweese

SUNDAY SCHOOL SUPERINTENDENTS METHODIST CHURCH
(FROM AVAILABLE RECORDS)

1870	G. A. Simpson — S. S. Vosburg
1871	W. Beard — S. S. Vosburg
1872	W. Beard — W. W. Mount
1873	W. W. Mount — S. S. Vosburg
1874	W. W. Mount
1875	S. T. Dial
1879	Charles Peckenpaugh
1880	W. E. Kugler (minister)
1881	Acomb
1882	W. H. Queal
1883	W. N. Williams — A. Connett
1884	W. H. Queal
1884-1886	A. Connett
1887	S. B. Queal — William Vaughn
1888	A. Connett — S. B. Queal
1890	Mrs. Henry Stokes — A. Connett
1891	G. R. Clark — S. B. Queal
1892	H. C. Thompson
1893	W. P. O'Hara
1893-1894	S. B. Queal
Aug. 1894	Charles Peckenpaugh
1895	S. B. Queal
1896	Charles Peckenpaugh
1897	William F. Allen
1897-1898	S. B. Queal
1899-1908	William F. Allen
1911	Fred Leever
1912-1918	Charles Boyd
1919-1923	S. B. Quayle
1924-1932	Wilber Myers
1933	Mrs. Strong
1934-1941	Wilber Myers
1941-1946	Clarence Oligee
1946-1948	James Morris
1949-1951	Wesley Rahn
1952	James Morris
1954	Margaret Schmidt
1955	Richard Leever
1956	Frank Tingley

INDEX

Abbott, Dr. 45
Adams, Margaret Glazier 54
Alim 23
Allen, William 45
Anderson, David 45, 46
Anderson, John 46
Ausmann, Charles 108
Barrels 13
Bates, General Joshua 30
Baumheckel, Frank 50
Barrere, Joseph 47
Bauer, John 47
Beard, William 33, 73, 74
Benken, August 48, 49
Bennett, Robert 45
Bollender, Elizabeth 8
Borgerding, Henry 50
Boy Scouts of America 104
Boyd, Charles 50
Bradley, Mrs. Ramona Kaiser 105
Brauneis, Enrich. J. 74
Broadus, Marshall 44
Brown, Conrad 49
Brown, William 52
Brunner, Chrif 49
Bryant, Alfred 49
Buckingham, Dr. Alfred 18, 29, 87
Buckingham, Enoch 17
Buckingham, Horatio 75, 77
Buckingham, Levi 7, 17
Buckingham, Marcia 77, 79
Buckingham, Sarah Vandiver 77-81
Buckingham, Smith 71, 73, 74
Buildings and Residences 118, 119
Bush, Fred 49
Callendar, Nathaniel C. 73
Campbell, Eleazer 71
Camp Dennison 27
Camp Dennison Building Ass'n 40
Camp Dennison Concrete Block Co. 105
Camp Dennison Today 116
Camp Meetings, Methodist Church.. 70
Camp Ross 104
Carter, Harry 50, 105
Cartwright, Peter 69
Case, George 50
Cedar Banks 31
Chalfont, Charles 108
Chicamauga 33
Church, earliest 12
Cincinnati, Milford & Blanchester Traction Co. 102
Circuit Riders 69
Cisco, Crawford 44
Civil War 69
Clement 29
Cochran, Charles 50, 51
Cochran, Fred 51
Cocker Spaniel Kennel 65
Codderman, Adan. 8
Codderman, Conrad 8
Compton Rebecca 51
Connett, Maria Queal 23
Cordes, Henry 51
Cox, General Jacob D. 30
Cullom, George 52
Cunningham, Albert 17
Cunningham, William 17
Custard, Magdalena 15
Daughters, Charles 52
Daughters of American Revolution.. 105
Davis, William 45
de Golyer, Antoni 8
Deweese, Raymond 79
Distillery 9
Doermann, Emma Fletcher 79

Doty, Arthur 52
Drake, Samuel 52
Ebbert, Isaac 71
Eberhardt, William 52
Edsall, Charles 26
Edwards, Harley 113
Elections, Community House 78
Electric Service 102
Elliott 52
Elstun, Clarence 113
Eltzroth, Roy 108
Falgner, Leo 108
Faul, Joseph 52
Faul, Nicholas 25
Ferguson, A. E. 29
Ferguson, Charles 113
Filling Station 105
Fischer, August W. 53
Fitzwater, Thomas 8
Fletcher, Hall 55, 56
Fletcher, William 18
Fletcher, David 18
Fletcher, Jesse 18
Flint, Albert 75, 103
Forward, Samuel 53
4-H Clubs 103
4-H Club Leaders 104
Frankenbert, Henry 108
Frazier, William 45
Frieberger, Ludwig 8
Fry, Hereward 53, 76, 77
Fry, Sylvester 53, 54
Fulling Business 10
Gant, Harry E. 109
Gant, William 53
German Reformed Church 69
General Store 41
Germany 21-26
Glazier, Margaret 54
Grand Valley 38
Grand Valley Sunday School 83
Granite Improvement Co. 41
Green, Charles A. 54
Greene, Robert 108
Gristmill 9
Haffenbradl, Joseph 54, 75
Haller, Herman 111
Hancock, Porter 54
Harner, George 7
Hartzell, Benson 55
Heaton, Daniel 55
Hermann, George D. 74
Herr, William 70
Hillard, Mary 109
Hodges, Frank 55
Holmes, James H. 81, 90
Hospital, Union 27
Howell, Earl Sr. 109
Hunter, Booker T. 114
Jackson, Clifford 75, 103
Keith, T. 71
Keller, John 12
Kennedy, Robert 105
Kindt, Elmer 109
Kinney, John 55
Kizer, A. J. 56
Knicely, William B. 56
Kroger, Chester 105
Krome, John 57
Kugler House 10
Kugler, John 21, 71, 72
Kugler, Matthias 9, 21, 71
Kugler Mill Road 21
Ladies Aid Society 77
Lang, John 57
Laudeman, Albert 109

153

Leckie, Hans	8
Leever, Fred	57
Leever, Hiram	74
Leiman, Edward	57
Lewis, Arthur	57
Lewis, Ed	57
Library	42
Little, John	57
Little Miami Railroad	21, 22
Lockwood, James	109
Longley, Cyrenius	58
Ludlow, Edward	56
Lytle, General M. H.	31
McAfee, Charles	58
McClain, Orville	114
McCook, Daniel	31
McCook, General Robert	31
McGohan, Clem	59
McGohan, George	59
McGohan, James H.	59
Malott, George	110
Malott, Leroy	110
Mammoth Tusks	105
Marsh, George	59
Martin, Joseph	109, 110
Methodist Church, Chapter V	69-86
Methodist Church, Bible Classes	80
Methodist Church, Building of	71
Methodist Church, Epworth League	85
Methodist Church, Fire	79
Methodist Church, First Organ	82
Methodist Church, Milford	69
Methodist Church, Minister	79
Methodist Church, Moving of, 1868	74
Methodist Church, Musical Organization	80
Methodist Church, Pianists	80-81
Methodist Church, Singing Club	80
Methodist Church, Sunday School	81-84
Methodist Church, Trustees	71, 74, 79
Methodist Church, Women's Society of Christian Service	85
Methodist Church, Young People's Organization	85
Meyer, Joseph H.	59
Miami Exporting Company	10
Milford Methodists	71
Millcroft Inn	21
Mills, William	59, 60
Mintkenbaugh, Joseph	60, 61
Montag, Johannes	16
Moore, Percy	60
Morgan, John	31
Morgan's Raid	32
Morris, James	109
Mt. Olivet Baptist Church	42
Myers, Clark C.	110
Nelcamp, John H.	61
O'Hara, W. P.	61, 85, 89
Ohio Gravel Co., The	105
Ohio Homes, Inc.	79, 107
Ohio National Guard	104
Packard, H.	71
Paper, manufacture of	11
Peckenpaugh, Charles	16
Peckenpaugh, Frederick	16, 74
Peckenpaugh, Frederick Jr.	16
Peteler, Frank	61
Pierce, Charles	60
Pinkvoss, Henry F.	61, 62
Pinkvoss, Henry M.	62
Pinkvoss, Louis	63
Pinkvoss, Rolf	61
Pitser, Henry	111
Pond, Stanley	63
Price, Daniel	18
Price, Jeremiah	18, 71, 73, 74
Price, Nimrod	18, 23
Quarterly Conferences, Methodist Church	70
Quayle, Smith B.	24, 67, 77, 84
Queal, George W.	23
Queal, John O.	24
Queal, Michael	23
Queal, William Henry	23, 34, 81
Queal, William	77
Quinn, Charles	110
Rabe, Walter	110
Radcliffe, Fred	55
Rahn, August	111
Rahn, C. Wesley	111
Rahn, George August	111
Rammler, Theodore	63
Recent Growth	107
Rededication of church 1926	69, 77
Reese, William	63
Reich, Thomas	8
Reservoir	30, 31
Ritchie, James	111
Robe, Russell	110
Robinson, Henry	114
Robinson, Lee	63
Robinson, Sam	63
Robinson, Tom	63
Rosecrans, General W. S	29
Ruff, Alice	64
Ruff, Ella	64, 75, 80
Sawmill	9
Schmidt, Charles	64
School, Chapter VI	87-100
School Building, 1863	87
School, First Building	87
School in Community House, 1938	78
School, Indian Hill, 1950	88
School, Remodeled 1939	88
School, Sale of Building	89
School, Names of Teachers	89
Schroeder, Herman	63
Schwey, Rose	50
Secrest Monument	35
Shively, Everett	64
Simpson, George	73, 74, 87
Singleton, Homer	111
Smith, John	11
Stinette, Guy	112
Store, Waldsmith	12
Stroman, Henry	69, 71, 73
Strong, James	111, 112
Subdivisions	38, 39
Sunday School Conventions	84
Sunday School Library	84
Sunday School, Members of, 1870	82
Symmes Township	117
Taverns	41
Taylor, Vernon	112
Telephone Service	42
Telgmann, Theodore	62
Terwilleger, John	17
Theil, Dr. Jacob	65
Thompson, Bessie	84
Thompson, Hamilton C.	66
Tingley, Eugene	64
Tittle, Leonidas	39, 64
Two More Wars, Chap. VII	101
Turner, William	112
Tyler, Richard	112
U. S. Post Office	41
Van Pelt, Emma	78
Vosburg, S. S.	74, 81, 82
Waits, George E.	65
Waldsmith House, DAR Museum	105, 118
Waldsmith, Christian	7-16, 69, 87
Waldsmith House	10
Waldsmith, Peter	10, 11
Walls, Bert	65
Walsh, Thomas	25
Walton, George	43
Walton, Louis	43, 105
Walton, Morris	43, 105

War Between the States	27
War, 1917	101
War, 1917, Soldiers Serving in	101
War, 1941	101
War, 1941, Ladies Auxiliary, Red Cross	102
War, 1941, Soldiers Serving in	101
Ward, William	112
Wartnaby, Sarah Southworth	64
Washington Survey Purchase	14
Water Supply	104
Weaver, Henry	112
Weber, Richard	65
Westerkamm, Louis	112
White, John	114
Whitelock, William	66, 75
Wiggins, Jeanetta	113
Wiley, Edward	65
Wiley, Minor	77
Williams, E. E.	66
Williams, Enos	114
Williams, Perry	114
Williamson	72
Women's Society of Christian Service	79
Worsham, William	44
Yeast Production	53
Zumstein, John	34